FAR CAPE ™

THE ILLUSTRATED SEASON 2 COMPANION

FARSCAPE: THE ILLUSTRATED SEASON 2 COMPANION

1 84023 308 7

Published by
Titan Books
A division of
Titan Publishing Group Ltd
144 Southwark St
London
SE1 0UP

First edition June 2001
10 9 8 7 6 5 4 3 2 1

Photographs supplied by The Jim Henson Company,
Farscape Productions and Ruth Thomas.

ACKNOWLEDGEMENTS
The authors would like to thank the following for their help in turning round this book so easily: Anthony Winley and Lesley Parker for allowing us to spend time on the set at Homebush Bay; all of those we interviewed for so graciously giving up their time; our partners, Alison and Julian, for allowing us to abandon them for three weeks while we travelled to the other side of the planet; Sinead Bennett, Rod Edgar, David Hughes and Tony Tatman for their help in the preparation of the manuscript; Adam Newell, David Barraclough, Jo Boylett, Oz Browne and Duncan Brown at Titan; and especially Rockne S. O'Bannon and David Kemper for once again being available for questions and discussion despite all the many other calls on their time.

DEDICATION
For Mel Goodwin. It's all your fault!

What did you think of this book? We love to hear from our readers. Please e-mail us at: readerfeedback@titanemail.com or write to Reader Feedback at the address above.

Titan Books are available from all good bookshops or direct from our mail order service. For a free catalogue or to order, phone 01858 433169 with your credit card details, e-mail asmltd@btinternet.com or write to Titan Books Mail Order, Bowden House, 36 Northampton Road, Market Harborough, Leics, LE16 9HE. Please quote reference FS/C2.

A CIP catalogue record for this title is available from the British Library.

Printed and bound in Great Britain by MPG, Bodmin, Cornwall.

FARSCAPE

THE ILLUSTRATED SEASON 2 COMPANION

Paul Simpson and Ruth Thomas

Series created by Rockne S. O'Bannon

TITAN BOOKS

CONTENTS

Seldom in this industry do we get an opportunity to create something truly unique. Broadcasters are often concerned that they will "miss" their audience if they are too bold in their programming. This can be a major stumbling block when trying to launch something like *Farscape*. It took five years for a broadcaster to emerge with the courage to commission the show. SCI FI's original order of twenty-two episodes was the green light for hundreds of creative geniuses (perhaps even lunatics) in London, Los Angeles and Sydney to let rip!

What they created is a science fiction series that breaks all the rules of science fiction. Indeed, if there is any rule to *Farscape*, it is that there are no rules. As we moved into season two, more than ever, this shifting reality forced our main characters to often question their own morality, sexuality, even their sanity.

Every episode leans entirely on the strength of the characters to pull the story along. This allows the characters and their relationships to develop in a much more exotic way than we are used to seeing in science fiction. With the blessing of an extraordinary cast, the show has been able to become the

first adult science fiction series with a sense of humour and the courage to be outrageous.

Starting as the brainchild of Rockne S. O'Bannon, and continuing as the playground for David Kemper, *Farscape* has become the testing ground for Australia's top directing talent. Bring into the mix incredible production design, creature effects and visual effects, and you get a series like nothing we've ever seen on television. Each episode is a mini-movie bursting with ingenuity that puts to shame most Hollywood feature films.

Having been to the Los Angeles *Farscape* Convention in August 2000, I was thrilled to see that most of you are as insane as we are. Keep it up, *Farscape* has only just begun!

Brian Henson

Brian Henson
May 2001

Rockne S. O'Bannon

"We were real proud of what we did in season one, and we were trying to figure out how we did it, recreate it, and then top it in season two."

EXT. SPACE — ON CRICHTON AND D'ARGO FLOATING (CG)

CRICHTON

It may not matter…
(beat)
D'Argo's lost consciousness…

As Crichton reaches over to touch his friend, his father's good luck charm comes free from their grasp, and IT FLOATS GENTLY AWAY.

Then, as we PUSH CLOSE on Crichton's reaction to everything…

THE END OF SEASON ONE

lthough the writers of *Farscape* knew how they were going to rescue Crichton and D'Argo from their perilous position at the end of the first season, there were more practical points that had to be dealt with by the show's producers before filming could begin. By far the most important of these was finding a new home for the series.

Season one had been shot at Fox Studios, right in the heart of Sydney, but there had been problems from the start. *Farscape* is a large production and it had constantly needed to spread. "We had to dismantle sets to make room for other sets the whole time," actor Anthony Simcoe recalls. "We had to lose sets we didn't want to lose. The first casualty was the command deck from the Peacekeeper Cruiser. No one wanted to lose it, but it went because we didn't have time to keep taking it down and putting it up again."

"Half the reason we left Fox was because they booked up our studio space for *Star Wars Episode II* and *Moulin Rouge*," executive producer David Kemper says. "The other half was because we simply needed *more* space than the three tiny sound stages we were originally allowed. Also, we needed tons more space than was available for the Creature Shop, Make-up, Construction, and all the rest."

"We always had to move," incoming line producer Anthony Winley adds. "There was a proposition at one point to move out and construct our

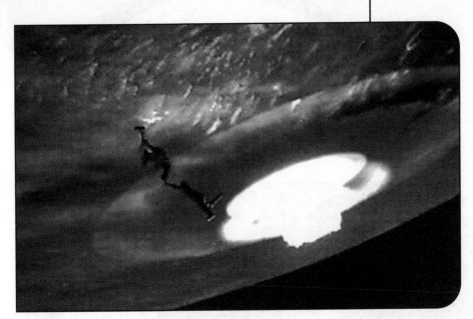

own studio. We would have taken over a warehouse and built our own stages. There would have been three, which in hindsight would have been inadequate."

Renowned Australian film and television producer Sue Milliken joined the show for the second year. "When Matt Carroll decided not to carry on as producer on the second season, I was asked to take over," she recalls. "It's such a big show, and in a town like Sydney, which is not built around film like Los Angeles is, finding a new home was a bit of a challenge. So moving the show to the studio we chose, at Homebush Bay, getting everybody settled down, and creating a good strong productive working environment for season two was quite a job. There were some initial problems, but we soon got a good team spirit going."

There were some changes on camera as well. "We moved from one visual effects house to another, but the transition wasn't difficult," Tony Winley says. "It was by no means acrimonious: Garner McLellan made a decision not to do any more work on the show and we moved it to Animal Logic. We got all the basic computer generated elements for Moya and so on and took them over, but we had to do all the texturing and stuff again. That was great because it meant Animal Logic could put their signature look on it straight away."

With the cast and crew now making the daily journey out to Homebush — next to what was then the construction site for the 2000 Olympics — the filming of season two could get underway...■

Above: Season one's exciting climax: Crichton and D'Argo are stranded in space.

THE EPISODES

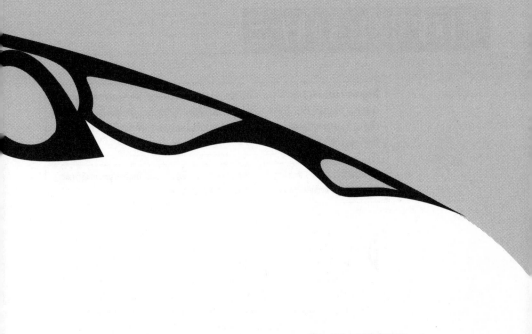

"Best I can do is tell you what I saw. No coverings, no editorials,

no axes to grind. Does that work for you?"

– John Crichton

MIND THE BABY

Regular cast: Ben Browder (John Crichton), Claudia Black (Aeryn Sun), Anthony Simcoe (Ka D'Argo), Virginia Hey (Zotoh Zhaan), Gigi Edgley (Chiana), Tim Mieville and team (Rygel: movement), Jonathan Hardy (Rygel: voice) Sean Masterson and team (Pilot: movement), Lani Tupu (Pilot: voice)

Written by: Richard Manning
Directed by: Andrew Prowse

Guest cast: Lani Tupu (Crais), Wayne Pygram (Scorpius), David Franklin (Lt Braca)

D'Argo awakes from a nightmare to discover that he and Crichton have been rescued from certain death by Aeryn, who has brought them to an uninhabited asteroid with an oxygen atmosphere. Unknown to them, however, she has formed an alliance with Crais and is helping him train Moya's offspring, Talyn. Meanwhile, on board Moya, Chiana, Rygel and Pilot debate the wisdom of Moya's decision to look for Talyn. Scorpius, on his Command Carrier, admits that his intention was for Aeryn to rescue Crichton, but then be captured, and he's annoyed that she evaded him. On the asteroid, Crichton and D'Argo are confused by Aeryn's abrupt and aggressive attitude. Crichton forces her to admit to her deal with Crais, at which point D'Argo knocks her out. Crichton heads after Crais, who at that moment is submitting a progress report to Scorpius regarding his manipulation of the situation…

Crais to Scorpius

"Demonstrate some of the formidable patience you're always bragging you possess."

"My patience is formidable, Crais. But it is not infinite."

"The actors had something they could get their teeth into," says supervising producer Andrew Prowse, who also directed the first episode of season two to be broadcast ('Dream a Little Dream' was actually filmed first).

"Ricky Manning said he'd write it," executive producer David Kemper recalls, "then it became a big joke because once he had his hands on it, he was calling up and saying, 'What the hell do I do now?'"

"Wrap-up episodes are hard to do," Andrew Prowse confirms, "simply because you've got to tie up a load of loose ends. There's often an air of anticlimax in doing that, but I think we got over that with 'Mind the Baby'."

The episode had a more dialogue-driven script than some, allowing the drama to unfold between the actors. "I think Andrew Prowse enjoyed it," Claudia Black says, "because he came from a gritty Australian police drama, *Wildside*, with its particular acting style: you loosely follow the script and improvise in the moment. With Ben Browder, Anthony Simcoe and me doing all of those scenes on the asteroid, it was closer to theatre in some ways."

"It was one of those rare moments you get when you're not totally exhausted and you have a lot of time," says Andrew Prowse of this early part

of the season. One of the benefits of that extra time was the creation of
Scorpius's cooling rod. "*Farscape* is so flexible," Prowse adds. "The show is
so organic that the cooling rod became a key element to the end of the season. It's a beautiful example of how *Farscape* works. It feeds on its own creative resources."

The brief that Manning was given was to "figure out a way of making
Crais part of the team, and yet keep the level of mistrust for him," David
Kemper says, "so that the audience wasn't positive what Crais could do for
Moya's crew. Then he had to humanise the characters a little bit." 'Mind the
Baby' accordingly allowed Scapers to see a fresh side to the series' chief villain. "Scorpius now has relationships with other people," Prowse says. "He
has a relationship with Braca and he has the possibility that he's vulnerable.
It humanised our villain and made him more interesting. What do you do
when you've invented evil incarnate? You have to find his weak spots. You
have to find a way for our hero to deal with him. You have to open the chink
in Scorpy's armour."

Other new elements came into play during the episode: we see the possibility of Aeryn betraying her shipmates to Crais, as well as offering to leave
with Talyn. "She gets caught in this conflict of how to protect Talyn," Ben

Above: Aeryn and
Crais battle for
control of Talyn.

Next page: Aeryn
watches as Crais takes
command.

Browder recalls, "and at the end of it Crichton thinks Aeryn's going to go, but she doesn't." Talyn chooses to offer the computer's symbiotic link, the Hand of Friendship, to Crais. "We had to build the Hand," Sydney Creature Shop creative supervisor Dave Elsey recalls. "It's a revamp of something we did on Jotheb in the first season's 'Throne for a Loss'. We took the skin off his mechanical tentacles and realised that we couldn't build anything that looked as good as that. So we adapted it and made it look a little bit more Peacekeeperish."

Andrew Prowse reveals a small piece of trivia that made its way into the episode: "The scissors-paper-stone gag with D'Argo was a nice idea. You have Crichton and D'Argo playing it, and then it's reprised later, with D'Argo playing it with himself. Fans know that D'Argo has two of everything — two brains, two hearts — so he can actually play the game with himself!" ∎

≡ VITAS MORTIS

Written by: Grant McAloon	Guest cast: Melissa Jaffa (old Nilaam), Anna Lise Phillips
Directed by: Tony Tilse	(young Nilaam)

umours of a Luxan female bring Crichton, D'Argo and Zhaan to a desolate planet, where the female, Nilaam, resides inside a foreboding castle, awaiting death. When she addresses D'Argo as General and he realises that she is an Orican, he is alarmed and starts to leave. Nilaam calls him back, and he offers to attend her in her death ritual. Zhaan tells Crichton that an Orican is a Luxan holy woman. Nilaam tests and rejects D'Argo, hurling him backwards out of the room, and he, ashamed, explains why he has the markings of a general. Crichton and Zhaan reassure him that he is not a fraud, so he reiterates his offer to Nilaam, claiming that if she is not interested in his explanation, then he isn't the only fraud. D'Argo tells his friends that it is an honour to assist in an Orican's rit-

Crichton

" D'Argo, just because some ancient Luxan doesn't like the feel of your spleen does not mean she has the right to call my friend a fraud! "

ual of passing, but an argument ensues when Crichton discovers the ceremony could be fatal to D'Argo. However, the Luxan's mind is made up. During the ritual, instead of dying, Nilaam is unexpectedly rejuvenated, with catastrophic consequences for Moya…

"We wanted to give D'Argo a big show, and a love story," David Kemper explains. "We know that he is superstitious, so let's explore that and bring in a witch." But making such an episode caused problems for the director. "'Vitas Mortis' was hard because it had sex and a suicide which you couldn't see," Tony Tilse recalls. Farscape's first on-screen sex scene, between D'Argo and Nilaam, caused practical problems because of D'Argo's make-up. "Really basic things influenced that scene," Anthony Simcoe remembers. "When I'm in the make-up, I can't really lie down, and if I do, I can't move. I have to be set in place, which unfortunately doesn't lend itself to the most creative way to show alien sex! I had pillows stuffed behind my back, so I could give the impression I was lying back a little. Then we had to make it sexy and fun. That scene really sells itself through the reactions on the other people's faces rather than what's going on within the shot itself."

Nilaam's suicide was also problematical. "You don't want to go down a path of goriness," Tony Tilse explains, "so we came up with the idea of the blood running down the sword that crystallised and then exploded." One idea that didn't make it to the screen was that "the crystal exploded into a whole lot of lights that became stars. We'd be in space, and the crew would realise that Nilaam has entered another realm."

Unusually for this kind of story, the two versions of Nilaam were played by different actors, rather than one person being made to look older or younger as the scenes required. "It was really hard to find two that would match," Tilse says. "We ultimately had to voice it all with one actor's voice — it was too hard to get your head around Nilaam having two different voices. Melissa Jaffa's voice was used, since she appeared first and we were used to her voice."

Creating female Luxans was another challenge for Dave Elsey. "We were given two weeks to create them," he recalls. "However, we'd never seen a female Luxan before. Having seen Anthony and the way his make-up goes together before the beard goes on, you realise that half the Luxan is the beard. Take that off and it looks quite peculiar. It doesn't seem to work if you take away one aspect of it."

Consequently, Elsey decided that Luxan women would look very different from the men. "The first thing we had to lose was the chin: it definitely did not work without the beard," Elsey says. "Then we lost the beard as well. As anyone who's seen *Monty Python's Life of Brian* will tell you, women with beards don't work! We decided it was another opportunity to do something with the tentacles because D'Argo's tentacles are always

worn down. I thought they were like Luxan hair, and it would be inter-esting if Nilaam wore the tentacles up on her head. So we would need some form of framework to support that." The script's description of Nilaam as a Luxan holy woman also influenced the design. "We wanted her to look slightly formidable, like a mediaeval shaman."

While D'Argo is busy on the planet, Chiana is stuck in Moya's amnexus fluid. "It was a piece of acrylic with two circles cut out which I put my feet in," Gigi Edgley recalls. "There was some room at the back, so in all the scenes I had to push my legs forward. It was a bit uncomfortable and I ended up getting a few grazes — but it's all in a day's work. It's fantastic when you're put in a physical lock like that. It does become real. I could use that frustration."

"We created that story to have ready in the trunk to give Anthony Simcoe something special to do," David Kemper notes. "When we were working on the last four stories of season one, Grant McAloon didn't have another script to write for that year. I suggested to him that he should start working on a script for the next season, although at that stage I didn't know if we were going to be coming back. I bought the script from him anyway. It could have played any-where, but it was ready, so we put it up second in the year." ∎

Opposite page:
Nilaam puts D'Argo
to the test.

Above: *D'Argo*
and a rejuvenated
Nilaam.

Written by: Justin Monjo	Guest cast: Anthony Hayes (Molnon), Peter Scarf (Das),
Directed by: Rowan Woods	Michela Noonan (Vyna), Natasha Beaumont (Janixx)

A fter Crichton dismisses her because he's too busy to talk, a distraught Chiana goes to the maintenance bay and surgically removes a pulsating object from her abdomen, which slows, then stops. Stealing Aeryn's Prowler, Chiana heads for a nearby cemetery planet, where she is attacked by a trio of adolescents. Back on Moya, Zhaan recognises the object as a life disc whose dormant state indicates the death of someone linked with Chiana. Following the young Nebari to the planet, Rygel indulges in a spot of grave-robbing, while Crichton and Aeryn search underground, eventually discovering Chiana suspended upside down, surrounded by the youths. When they try to rescue her, Chiana responds aggressively, telling them to leave her alone. The youths react with disdain to Crichton and Aeryn, referring to them as ancients. Members of their clan don't survive past the age of twenty-two. Their society revolves around hallucinogenic fungi and ultimate thrill-seeking. Not caring whether she lives or dies, Chiana tells Crichton and Aeryn that she wants to participate in the most risky of all the youths' rituals: Taking the Stone...

Crichton to Aeryn

"Be nice"

"I'm not good at nice."

"Just don't shoot her."

"Justin Monjo was freaked by Gigi and Chiana," David Kemper explains. "He wanted to write a Chiana episode, and he had a very clear vision of this culture of people who were dying young. He wanted to do thrill-seekers." The "dropheads", as costume designer Terry Ryan describes them, took the series into new ground, as the episode tackled the theme of recreational drug use. "To me it seemed we'd created a world that was actually quite sophisticated," producer Sue Milliken points out, "and the way that world operated was at an adult level. It's easier to tell more interesting stories if you have that ingredient of adult themes. I think that it really enhances the show."

Monjo also incorporated an idea from series creator Rockne S. O'Bannon's visit to an old cemetery on his first trip to Australia. "It was on a hillside that goes all the way down to a cliff, down to the ocean," O'Bannon recalls. "If you stood at the top of this really extensive cemetery, and looked downwards, it seemed like a whole cemetery world."

Claudia Black enjoyed the battle between Crichton and Aeryn in the episode. "I just liked the opportunity to be in opposition to Crichton in a different way," she says, "for there to be conflict between the two of them brought about by a massive shift in their roles and their mindsets. It also gave

them more of an opportunity to be like parents quarrelling over an errant child. It's a nice reversal when Aeryn wants to use words rather than actions and Crichton is the one who's trying to knock Chiana out and drag her back to the ship."

Above: Molnon, Das and Vyna.

Next page: Chiana in the Sonic Cowl.

"It's not typical John behaviour," Ben Browder agrees. "I think in a lot of ways that episode is very, very good. John doesn't want Chiana to die. He thinks she's going to make a stupid decision, so he's going to do whatever he has to, do whatever he thinks is right. There's a side issue, which is that he's a little nuts! From the time he stepped out of the Aurora Chair in 'The Hidden Memory', he's actually been nuts. If you watch his reactions to situations, they're slightly off. I made the conscious choice that I was not going to react the way a normal person would react. John's synapses are in a weird place; he's sort of suffering from a mild schizophrenia. He's over-reacting to things he shouldn't react to, and he's under-reacting to things he should react to."

Browder suggested that Crichton should start to recognise that something is wrong. "Talking to Justin about the script, I said that I was a little worried because no-one was mentioning that Crichton was acting any way other than normal," he recalls. "So Justin added in Crichton asking, 'Lately,

do I seem a little crazy to you?' and Aeryn goes 'What do you mean, lately?' The rest of the crew hasn't really cottoned on to the fact that John is nuts. The audience hasn't cottoned on to it either."

With her circus training, Gigi Edgley loved the episode's stuntwork. "At university, I used to do trapeze stuff to make extra cash," she recalls. "There's a nice comfort in being up and away from the world. Doing the leap with the harness was like a big Christmas present. Taking the Stone at the end of the episode was even better because it was a bigger fall. It was great to do all of that."

For what was otherwise a light episode for the Creature Shop, Dave Elsey had to create an alien pregnancy. "We wanted to do a pregnancy which was different from any other. At first they wanted the baby on the girl's neck, like it was attached to her, but didn't want it to look unattractive. I pointed out that if you had a baby attached to the side of her neck, it was never going to be attractive, no matter what we did! So we came up with the idea that she would have a pregnant stomach that was see-through, so you could see the baby inside."

The alien worms that Rygel encounters delighted his voice artist, Jonathan Hardy, who enjoyed making the requisite Hynerian slurping noises. "I'm always pleased when Rygel has something wriggly to eat!" he laughs. ∎

Written by: Justin Monjo	Guest cast: Wayne Pygram (Scorpius), Danny Adcock
Directed by: Ian Watson	(Traltixx)

A trip to restock supplies is cut short when the crew discover that Scorpius has left Wanted Beacons on every Commerce planet. In desperation, D'Argo brings aboard a mechanic, Traltixx, who claims to be able to make Moya undetectable. Traltixx's heightened senses compensate for his blindness. Despite Crichton's misgivings, they test Traltixx's device successfully on *Farscape 1*. To get to Traltixx's home world to fit a full-size device to Moya, they must pass by five pulsars, and Traltixx warns that 'lesser species' will suffer some wooziness and a slight impairment of judgement. As they begin their journey, the crew start to squabble over the fair distribution of the crackers — the only food that they were able to obtain. It soon becomes clear that this is the smallest bone of contention in an increasingly disquieting and paranoid atmosphere, which is not helped by Traltixx's manipulation of Pilot...

> **Pilot to Crichton**
>
> "But do you trust him?"
>
> "Hell, no, I don't trust him. Do I look stupid to you? No, please, don't answer that question."

'Fear and Loathing in the Uncharted Territories,' is Gigi Edgley's nickname for 'Crackers Don't Matter', the episode which its director Ian Watson sees as the time when *Farscape* "went from its adolescence to its really dangerous young adulthood, having serious attitude." Line producer Anthony Winley regards it as his favourite of the year: "It was a lot of paranoid fun. There were a lot of laughs, so I just love it."

'Crackers Don't Matter' came about as a result of the sudden necessity for an episode that could take place entirely on board Moya. "Justin Monjo just went crazy with it," Rockne S. O'Bannon says. And he came up with a script that Lani Tupu regards as a "gift".

There were a number of comic moments during the episode. Claudia Black loves the showdown in Command between Crichton and Aeryn which

ENCOUNTERS: TRALTIXX

A blind lifeform with an insect-like ability to defy gravity and scuttle up walls and along ceilings. With heightened senses to counter-balance his blindness, the light from five pulsars can fuel him and other members of his currently dormant species. He can also shoot destructive light beams from the remnants of his eyes.

ends "absolutely ambiguously. The lights go down at the end, there's a charge and the sound of someone getting hit. We knew that we had to find Crichton dragging Aeryn in the next scene and it's nice to leave that up in the air."

However, it was not all humorous. "I love romps," Ben Browder states, "but I prefer it when there is also something which grounds the story." Crichton's attack on Chiana in the corridor is one such scene. "We shot that with the second unit about a week after I'd shot the whole episode," Ian Watson recalls. "I was looking at a rough-cut of it, and I thought that it hadn't gone dark enough. They were meant to really turn on each other."

"It was the first time I'd seen Ben really lose the plot," Gigi Edgley recalls. "It was a bit disturbing shooting it. It was very full on. I was really scared of him — you just don't see Ben like that. We were close range, one on one. There's this bizarre 'God knows what's going to happen next!' vibe. It's dark and crazy but it takes that madness to another level."

"I don't know if it was the mood that Ben was in or something, but it came out that way," Ian Watson adds. "The funny thing is, it was done with so much love and care from Ben to Gigi when we did it. They gave each other a big cuddle afterwards."

"We see that Crichton is capable of horrible things, and if he's capable

of horrible things, then him being good, honest, true and a boy scout is made more significant," Ben Browder points out. "It makes John real. That's one of those scenes which grinds the entire audience back to a sort of reality about the situation."

To face down Traltixx, John has to become Crichton the Ridiculous. "For me the crowning moment is when he gets up with vomit on his face, every bizarre thing, and goes for it," Rockne S. O'Bannon says. "Ben isn't afraid of image, of pushing too far. He trusts the process, trusts Andrew Prowse who looks after post-production, trusts David Kemper who oversees it all, and lets himself push it."

Ben Browder looks back at that scene and recalls thinking, "If I am going to fail, I'm going to fail gloriously. I would rather wear my mistakes and go down doing the worst thing in the history of the universe, than be mediocre. You strive to do cool, interesting stuff and some of it works, some doesn't."

Danny Adcock, who hung upside down looking through a periscope arrangement for the role of Traltixx, says, "You knew whatever discomfort you went through was worth it in the end. Having the journey that character made was so great." ∎

Opposite page:
*Traltixx joins the crew
on Command.*

*Above: Crichton
makes his point to
D'Argo and Chiana.*

PICTURE IF YOU WILL

Written by: Peter Neale **Directed by:** Andrew Prowse	**Guest cast:** Chris Haywood (Maldis and Kyvan)

hile Chiana and Rygel are browsing in a junkshop, the owner, Kyvan, insists on giving Chiana a picture, describing it as "a window into time". It suddenly changes to show Chiana wearing a necklace that she recently lost, and which a DRD passes to her when she returns to Moya. The painting changes again to show Chiana with a broken leg, as she falls to the ground with exactly that injury. Chiana thinks the painting can predict the future; D'Argo thinks the painting could be causing her problems and wants her to get rid of it, but he refuses. Zhaan is unsettled by the object, and tells Crichton that a time will come when she needs everyone to do what she says without question. Crichton agrees to back her up. Zhaan wants to destroy the painting, as it changes once again, this time showing Chiana on fire. The Nebari is placed in a freezer so she won't be able to burn, but, impossibly, she is engulfed by flames. When the crew get the door open, Chiana has gone...

> **Crichton**
> "I say we lock all of Moya's doors, we don't let anybody in, we don't let anybody out. That way we get no alien critters, no shape-shifting bugs, no mind-altering viruses, no freaky-deaky artifacts."

The idea at the centre of 'Picture If You Will' had been in David Kemper's head since 1985, when he'd read an article called 'Slow Glass', about a painting which could predict the future. For *Farscape*, he combined this with the concept behind W. W. Jacobs's classic horror story 'The Monkey's Paw', in which an object curses its owner. "As we developed it in the story sessions, we figured it was a good vehicle to bring Maldis back, and it just evolved," Kemper says.

The episode marked the début of Tim Ferrier as the series' production designer. "We were in the middle of the transition from Ricky Eyres to Tim," Kemper remembers. "He was looking around and wondering what the hell he had stepped into. For a while he didn't know how much latitude he could have. He didn't have a clue how free we will allow our creative people to be if they come up with something. Finally he came up with the idea of how to visualise the crew when they're trapped within the painting. When we saw what he had in mind, that's when we knew Timmy was good. First shot out of the bag, he nailed it."

"That had some great visuals in it," director Andrew Prowse recalls. "Conceptually I liked it, and that is reflected in some of the computer-generated images. We turned what were ostensibly real things into two-dimensional images, which was interesting and cool. We had to shoot for eight days

in a swimming pool! There was water on the floor in nearly every shot."

"It was a very difficult set to shoot in," Claudia Black agrees. "Lovely in design but acoustically very difficult." This meant that virtually every line of dialogue had to be re-recorded by the actors in a process called ADR (Additional Dialogue Recording) to remove any extra sounds that shouldn't be there.

The script involved more than the usual amount of visual effects, which made the filming process even more fragmented than normal. "The more visual effects you chuck in," Andrew Prowse points out, "and the more complex they are, the more frustrating it is to shoot. Not just technically, but from a performance point of view as well. The biggest problem Chris Haywood had as Maldis was working out what was going on. It was all shot in little bits. You can't get all the actors in that scene to interact with each other. You're interacting with a stationary image, and in that sense it's really hard to judge performance and get that dynamic going."

As well as seeing the return of Maldis from the first season's 'That Old Black Magic', the episode revisited the special bond that exists between Crichton and Zhaan after they shared Unity in season one's 'Rhapsody in Blue'. "If Zhaan says something to John, he'll accept it,"

Above: Maldis turns his back on Zhaan.

Next page: Kyvan shows the painting to Chiana and Aeryn.

Virginia Hey says. "If it was anyone else, he'd be dubious. But when Zhaan says he's got to do something, there's no question."

Ben Browder thinks Crichton is allowing other people to play to their strengths. "Zhaan is the only one on the ship who has a semblance of calmness about her," he says. "When things start to go really weird, that's Zhaan's department. John is smart enough to recognise the fact that this is her speciality. This is her deal, not his — it's not down to him to make the decision."

Physically, 'Picture If You Will' proved demanding for Virginia Hey. Shooting the scene where Maldis steps on Zhaan's head was somewhat uncomfortable for the actress. "He was wired up. He was in a harness underneath his costume and they had the crane holding him up. I think they gave him a little bit too much weight, because when he was walking on my head it was actually a bit painful. I didn't want to say anything at the time because I didn't want to seem a wimp!

"I did a bit of wire work in that episode as well," Hey adds, "but you didn't see it. It was a shame, because they had me flying about forty feet in the air and coming down at a real pace. You only ever saw the last foot, but in fact I was dropped from a massive height." ∎

Written by: Naren Shankar	**Guest cast:** Alex Dimitriades (Lt Velorek),
Directed by: Tony Tilse	Lani Tupu (Crais)

hiana shows Crichton a Peacekeeper recording she has found, revealing the murder of Moya's original Pilot, who had refused to co-operate with the Peacekeepers. A squad, including Aeryn Sun, gunned her down in cold blood. The group angrily confront Aeryn with the recording. She relates how three cycles earlier she was on a Leviathan — although she didn't know then it was Moya — when a new Pilot was brought aboard, bound and gagged. Lieutenant Velorek's mission was to bond the new Pilot with the Leviathan, and despite his abusive treatment of Pilot in front of Captain Crais, Velorek displayed an affection for the frightened creature. Moya's crew agree that Pilot should never see the recording. However, the tape has triggered memories for Aeryn of her doomed relationship with Velorek. When Rygel gives the recording to Pilot, it also triggers violent and disturbing memories for him. He summons, then physically attacks, Aeryn, before delivering an ultimatum: "until Aeryn leaves this vessel, Moya will not move another metra"…

> **Aeryn to Crichton**
>
> " You know, that time when he asked me to go with him, he said, 'You can be so much more.' That was exactly what you said to me on the first day I was here."

"Tony Tilse will try things that end up revolutionising the way we shoot *Farscape*, and everyone always responds so enthusiastically to what he does," Claudia Black says of the director of 'The Way We Weren't'. "This is the sort of episode you live for," Tilse explains.

"Naren Shankar had the idea of going back and doing Pilot's backstory and tying Aeryn in," David Kemper recalls. "He was fascinated by her, and wanted to do an Aeryn show as his first one. We told him it would be tough. It was a brutal exercise for Naren. He had to do many drafts to get to where it had to go. Then we did some staff work on it in the form of Rockne, but Naren laid all the groundwork. It turned out to be practically everybody's favourite episode, and that credit goes right back to Naren's original idea."

For the flashback sequences, Tilse used a film processing technique called bleach bypass. "When a film is developed, the silver on the film is exposed," he explains. "The film is bleached and most of the silver's washed off, but a certain amount is left on and it affects the film in a slightly organic way. It gave the set a grungy kind of look: when Moya was dominated by the Peacekeepers, I wanted her to look like a ship that had been seconded to the military."

Central to the story was Aeryn's relationship with Pilot. "I had an opportunity to go through every emotion there is on this show," Black recalls. "I would go home absolutely exhausted." For the scene where Aeryn is trying to release her aggression, the actress suggested a change of location: "Aeryn was supposed to be smashing her fist into a bulkhead in the side of Moya. Tony had difficulty with that because we're always aware that Moya is a living ship. I said that we'd had one other scene where Aeryn was boxing." Tilse realised how appropriate the location was when he saw that the gym mat bore the Peacekeeper emblem. When Aeryn subsequently pours out her heart to Crichton, "the mat symbolised so much of where she's from and what's keeping her apart from the others."

Pilot's puppeteers loved the episode. "We have to be so careful all the time when we're doing things on set," Sean Masterson explains. "When you get the chance and they say, 'Break out, go for it', everyone does. We were given *carte blanche* by the director, who asked to see the physicality of the puppet stretched to its limits."

Dave Elsey had to create a younger Pilot in somewhat less time than the nine months the original puppet took to make. "We had to adapt what we already had," he says. "We decided that the way to sell it to the viewer was to have his carapace much smaller, so there was a visible difference in the

way he looked. I also suggested that they should tweak Pilot's colours up in post-production, so he looked much more vibrant and younger. For his lower half, we had a spare body, which we turned upside down and stuck underneath Pilot's body. All we had to do was paint it and build a bunch of mechanical legs."

Unsurprisingly, this was Lani Tupu's favourite episode of the season. The moment when Crais first really notices Aeryn is one that Tupu had had in mind ever since the première: "Crais bursts in and sees Velorek and Aeryn. He sends Velorek out, then he looks back. I played it as, 'you're a very interesting, dedicated officer. I'll keep an eye on you.'" The story also allowed Tupu to show another side of Pilot: "He actually makes a decision about being on the ship. The scene with Velorek on the planet is one of my favourite scenes of the whole series." ■

Opposite page:
Velorek tempts Pilot on his homeworld.

Above: *Velorek connects Pilot to Moya.*

Written by: Gabrielle Stanton & Harry Werksman, Jr. Directed by: Rowan Woods	Guest cast: John Brumpton (B'Sogg), Justine Saunders (Altana), Rob Carlton (Vija), Hunter Perske (Temmon), Gavin Robins (Keedva)

Chiana brings Moya to the remains of a giant, inhabited space animal — a Budong — where she and her brother once spent some time. It's the crew's last hope of finding food, but they sense that Chiana is hiding something. Their hands are forced when Zhaan reveals that she must eat or die. An allergic reaction to Zhaan's illness sends Crichton, D'Argo, Chiana and Rygel off the ship to the Budong, leaving Aeryn to look after the Delvian. Their arrival coincides with a fatal accident in the Budong's mines, when an indigenous monster, the Keedva, attacks Chiana's contact, Temmon. Temmon's brother B'Sogg closes the mine and agrees to help everyone but Chiana obtain food, after they surrender their weapons.

Chiana is reunited with an old friend, Altana, who has found a rich seam of Nogelti ore and offers to share her fortune with the young Nebari, but they need to return to the mine to get at it. On board Moya, despite Aeryn's best efforts, Zhaan's condition is not only worsening, but also starting to affect the Leviathan, with disastrous results...

> **Aeryn to Crichton**
>
> "Oh, that's just great. I get to stay on board with the blooming blue bush and you get to play with your favourite little tralk."

"Aren't the writers amazing!" Virginia Hey exclaims about the concepts behind 'Home on the Remains'. "Where do they get these ideas from? They're such sick puppies!"

"This was another Chiana story," David Kemper says, "which didn't bother me at all, since it was a way of bringing her out and making her a very strong character." The script gave Gigi Edgley some more details about her character's past. "We get to meet her ex-boyfriend," she recalls. "I love Chi, but she does pick the most interesting boyfriends!" Rockne S. O'Bannon also liked the episode. "It's a good, solid mid-season story," he says. "It's got

ENCOUNTERS:
THE BUDONG AND THE KEEDVA

The Budong is one of the universe's largest creatures. Its flesh is filled with acid pustules and highly valuable Nogelti crystals, which are mined from its carcass after its death. The Keedva is a vicious cross between a large dog and an ape, which lives within and feeds off the Budong, or anything that gets in its way. It has a primitive learning capacity and can be trained to respond to simple commands.

Above: Chiana grieves over Altana's corpse.

Next page: Crichton threatens B'Sogg as Chiana looks on.

something that to me is very specific to *Farscape*. They're not on a planet or an asteroid, but the rotting carcass of a giant creature. They're mining inside this creature. In the grand scheme of science fiction stories it's not that wildly exotic, but it is in terms of television."

The miners within the Budong — or the "rubbish people" as costume designer Terry Ryan calls them — are deliberately reminiscent of the Gold Rush miners from the Yukon in the nineteenth century. The inspiration for the Keedva came from literature of the same period. "The first thing I thought of when I read the script was the Edgar Allen Poe story, 'The Murders in the Rue Morgue', which features a guy with an ape that's going round killing people," Dave Elsey recalls. "I was pleased with the way the creature was shot," he adds, referring to Rowan Woods' very effective 'less is more' approach — showing glimpses of the Keedva, rather than allowing the creature too much screen time.

John Brumpton featured in the episode as B'Sogg. "I had a great deal of fun doing it," the actor says. "Rowan and I were constantly looking for little sexual jokes within the story. All the sex stuff with Chiana gave it a little more depth. He wasn't just a bad guy trying to take over the mine. He had a history through Chiana and was trying to force her to give him a future.

"Rowan decided that modern accents didn't really work," Brumpton adds. "We wanted something really old, and the oldest accent I could do was an old Aboriginal. Unfortunately, an Aboriginal accent gets into similar territory to a bad American Deep South accent, so I had to come back and revoice a little bit of it, and pull it away from there."

Playing Aeryn's illness took Claudia Black back in time. "It was a lot of fun playing sick," she says. "I'd had plenty of practice at that when I was younger, and wanted to skip school. My parents are doctors, and I had to work very hard to prove to them that I was sick!" Black did need a little help to produce Aeryn's symptoms though: "Most of the time I prefer to produce the tears myself, but with fast turnaround television, if you can't do it, you can't do it. There's no shame in using a tear stick. However, it's so inorganic to blow menthol crystals into your eyeballs; you're not in control of the tears that produces. So for Aeryn's allergies, we just put some menthol under my eyes so there was an involuntary response. The sneezes and the coughs I obviously did, but there were feathers flying all around the set which reappeared for months afterwards!" ∎

DREAM A LITTLE DREAM

Written by: Steven Rae	Guest cast: Steve Jacobs (Ja Rhumann), Sandy Gore
Directed by: Ian Watson	(Judge), Simone Kessell (Finzzi), Marin Mimica (Dersch), Peter Kowitz (Tarr)

Zhaan awakes from a nightmare about Crichton's, Aeryn's and D'Argo's deaths. She and Crichton are stranded in a transport pod awaiting Moya's return, and while they wait, Zhaan relates to Crichton the events on Litigara which occurred after the Gammak Base's destruction… It's the twentieth planet that they have scoured for signs of their missing friends. Rygel is getting dren-faced, and Moya's patience is running out: she wants to search for Talyn. Zhaan crosses a street after a light has been deliberately changed, goading her into committing an offence, and she's arrested for the heinous crime of jaywalking. In jail, Zhaan begins to lose control of her emotions and sink into despair through her grief at the loss of her crewmates. Her court-appointed defender suggests that her sentence will be ten days' imprisonment, but Zhaan knows that Moya won't wait that long and attacks the attorney. Plagued by hallucinations of Crichton, Aeryn and D'Argo, the increasingly unstable Zhaan is offered a chance to escape, and takes it, but then stumbles over a body and is arrested for murder…

> **Rygel to Chiana**
>
> "I think I may have a way. It's chancy and will require lashings of deception and trickery."
>
> "Finally, you and I get to play to our strengths."

Although 'Dream a Little Dream' was broadcast eighth in the second season, it was actually the first episode before the cameras at Homebush Studios. "We didn't know where it was going to air," David Kemper explains. "We scripted an introductory teaser and a final tag shot for if it aired first, a teaser and a tag if it aired third, and another teaser and tag if it aired where it eventually aired. It had to reflect what the characters had gone through at that time. It was always planned as a moveable feast. It's actually very smart planning!"

ENCOUNTERS: LITIGARANS

Litigara is a planet of 90% lawyers, 10% utility workers. A simple book called *The Axiom* was the basis of their law, but as the number of lawyers increased, the book was expanded into an incomprehensible number of volumes to make it so complex as to justify their numbers. Lawyers became elevated to superior citizenship while the utility workers became second-class citizens with no rights. Any lawyer putting on a defence even suspected of being false shares their client's punishment.

The story's origins stretch back to 'The Inner Light', one of the initial scripts that Rockne S. O'Bannon prepared during the early development of *Farscape*, then known as *Space Chase*, back in 1994. "We took the concept of an existing script, and it was written again and updated," David Kemper explains. "The production vagaries were such that we were moving from Fox Studios to Homebush, and we would not have any Moya sets," O'Bannon adds. "They could build us a very simple guest location, but it had to be very specifically not Moya."

"We didn't feel we deserved the right to have a rest," Claudia Black says ruefully of her brief appearances in the story. "We ended up creating such an extraordinary pace to this series. It was odd to come back and shoot the first episode, and hardly be in it at all." Director Ian Watson did provide one of *Farscape*'s most memorable images: "One of my favourite shots is of Crichton, Aeryn and D'Argo walking down the corridor in slow-motion in silhouette," Black adds.

The focus of the episode was squarely on Zhaan, Chiana and Rygel. "It was Rygel as Rumpole of the Bailey and every other well-known trial lawyer," Jonathan Hardy recalls. "We went mad with the rhetoric in the trial. We worked like demons! Angus Robertson and I spent a long time in ADR

making sure the dramatic vocal lines made an impact, because it can make a hell of a difference to what is going on. Rygel really did have to set sail."

For the new Team Rygel puppeteers, the episode was a baptism of fire. "Not only did we come in as a new team to do Rygel," head puppeteer Tim Mieville says, "but Rygel was in about twenty-nine scenes, whereas normally he's in eight to fifteen. They doubled the workload, all the time saying it was a testimony to their faith in us. They didn't realise the hair that was being pulled out and the nails that were being bitten at our end. I think there's nothing like really going through the fires of Hell to know how to work something!"

Chiana's hyped-up performance in the trial chamber owed itself to "sugary drink after sugary drink to wire myself up for it," says Gigi Edgley. "My mouth was moving faster than the words were coming out. Then Ian said, 'Let's find different colours in the performance.' Chiana really was crazy!"

The framing sequence with Crichton and Zhaan in the transport pod saw a tuneful Ben Browder. "None of my singing in the entirety of season two was scripted," the actor points out. "What I like about it is that John is bringing a part of his world to an alien world. My voice is okay, singing *a cappella* in that scene," he adds modestly. ∎

Opposite page:
Chiana for the
Defence.

Above: *Zhaan in*
the dock.

OUT OF THEIR MINDS ≡

Written by: Michael Cassutt
Directed by: Ian Watson

Guest cast: Lani Tupu (Crais), Dominique Sweeney (Tak), Thomas Holesgrove (Yoz)

Crichton awakes to find that Moya is under attack by unknown assailants. Zhaan has shuttled over to the alien ship to negotiate peace, only to discover a scene of devastation, allegedly at the hands of Talyn. After Zhaan reassures a dying Halosian that Moya has no weapons, and is a ship of peace, the aliens drop the pretence that they were victims and resume their attack on the Leviathan. Rygel engages the defence screens as the Halosians fire, but instead of deflecting the energy weapon, it somehow distorts it, and on board Moya everyone's consciousness is propelled into another's body. Crichton's mind is now in Aeryn's body, Aeryn finds herself in Rygel's body, and the Hynerian suddenly has a human form to contend with. Things are no better in Pilot's chamber where D'Argo can't cope with being in Pilot. Pilot is in Chiana's body, which tries to reject him, while Chiana watches helplessly through D'Argo's eyes. D'Argo is unable to communicate with Moya and the Leviathan is floundering in space, with the Halosians planning a further attack...

> ### Crichton
> "Have we sent the 'don't shoot us, we're pathetic' transmission yet?"

"'Out of Their Minds' was a tremendous opportunity," Ben Browder says totally seriously. "Here I am on television pretending to be a puppet. Actors in the 'real world' don't get to do that. They can do it at drama school, but they don't get to do it on television or film!"

"I asked Mike Cassutt, who's a very old friend of mine, if he would help us out and do a script," David Kemper recalls. "He came in and we talked about body switching, which we'd never done on the show. I asked if he wanted to try a different episode, since this was an impossible one. 'No,' he said, 'let me give it a shot, and then you guys can take it over and do what you need to do.' That's what we did. Justin Monjo did a really good pass at it, took what Michael had laid down, and made it what we needed it to be for *Farscape*."

To make it work, director Ian Watson drew on his theatrical teaching background, organising sessions for the cast to practice swapping characters. "It was very easy to con everyone into doing those workshops," he jokes, "because they knew it would probably help. We did impersonation, copying and observation — standard character stuff."

"It was really great to get an insight into the other person's working process, because you had to articulate things that you've done instinctively or you've never had to articulate," Anthony Simcoe adds.

Everyone had specific areas that they concentrated on. "The difficulty with Rygel was trying to find a physicality that worked," Ben Browder says, "then Claudia and I had to agree on what we were going to do. Rygel has little arms. He doesn't know what to do with my body's arms, so he just keeps them in by his side."

Tapes of the lines that each actor performed for their counterpart dictated the puppeteers' performances as Rygel and Pilot. "If you're speaking with urgency, which Aeryn quite often does," Tim Mieville says, "she doesn't pad out the language that much. She doesn't use unnecessary words. Rygel is used to speaking with subtext the whole time, not being that honest, so we had to do more honest expressions and more concerned looks. With Crichton you've got all those human little bits you can throw in, and the Americanisms. We tried to get as many of those in as we could."

The original plan was that everyone would be overdubbed — when Ben Browder played Rygel, he would be overdubbed with Jonathan Hardy's voice. "I didn't think that was a good solution, because I didn't think it really tested the idea that they'd been swapped," Ian Watson says. "I rang a speech pathologist at Sydney University and found out theoretically what would happen if someone were to inhabit me. I would still sound the same way

Above: Zhaan tries to make Yoz see sense.

Next page: Rygel's body, but Aeryn's soul...

because it's my air passing over my vocal chords, so if Ben inhabited me, I'd be using some of his vocal ideas. I wouldn't have his accent; I'd still have my accent, but it would be influenced by the way he hears and says things."

Anthony Simcoe is proud of his scene with Ben Browder when he was playing Chiana in D'Argo's body, and Rygel was inhabiting Crichton. "We didn't rehearse that," he recalls. "We wanted to be fresh and launch into it. There was a lot of physical improvising going on during that actual take and I think that really played into our sense of trust. There's a lot of fun seeing two guys doing a scene like that. It was quite physically full on: Ben and I were right inside each other's spaces all the time, and it was quite sexual. For us as blokes to enter into that took a great deal of trust. That was fantastic. We both felt secure, so we could really make that scene play. It's one of my favourite scenes that I've ever done. I think it's detailed, interesting and funny. It's solid storytelling."

"We all had a big challenge on our hands to make that episode work," Claudia Black concludes, "but it does and I'm proud of it." ■

LOOK AT THE PRINCESS PART I: A KISS IS BUT A KISS

Written by: David Kemper
Directed by: Andrew Prowse & Tony Tilse

Guest cast: Wayne Pygram (Scorpius), Felicity Price (Princess Katralla), Bianca Chiminello (Jena), Matt Day (Tyno), Tina Bursill (Novia), Felix Williamson (Clavor), Aaron Cash (Dregon), Gavin Robins (Cargn), Francesca Buller (ro-NA), Jonathan Hardy (Kahaynu)

hen an intimate moment occurs between Crichton and Aeryn, she reacts badly and storms off. Moya is in orbit around a heavily defended world, and is told to leave by its representative, Councillor Tyno. Then Rygel steps in, using his royal status and diplomatic skills to ensure an invitation to the planet's upcoming coronation. After an argument with Aeryn, Crichton goes to invite Chiana down to the planet, only to find D'Argo and the young Nebari in a rather compromising position. Leaving Zhaan on Moya, the rest of the crew arrive on the planet to discover a civilisation where the mating ritual is solely dependent on a genetic compatibility test, which is conducted through a kiss. The crown's successor is in dispute as the rightful heir, Princess Katralla, must be married before succeeding, but has yet to find the necessary genetic match. This is the result of a plot by her younger brother Prince Clavor, who is in league with the Scarran Empire. Meanwhile, Scorpius's Command Carrier arrives at the planet's defensive perimeter and, hoping to decoy him away, Moya StarBursts. On the planet, Crichton is approached by Tyno, who requests that he kiss one more woman — Princess Katralla. When the test proves compatibility, the gathering is delighted. But Clavor is outraged, and his Scarran ally Cargn states that Crichton must die before the wedding can take place...

> **Crichton**
>
> "On my planet, we don't marry people we don't love, unless they're critically ill billionaires."

"'Look at the Princess' was a pretty ambitious little story," director Andrew Prowse says, with a very large degree of understatement. *Farscape*'s first three-part story had started life as a two-parter. "When Andrew finished shooting it," David Kemper explains, "we had eighteen minutes of extra footage left over. And it was good stuff. If it had been just a two-parter, we wouldn't even have had the time to show the wedding on screen. I was sitting with [line producer] Tony Winley, who said, 'Why don't you make it a three-parter?'" So after three weeks of plotting, Kemper threaded in eleven new scenes that would create the trilogy. "It was the most afraid I've ever been in television, waiting to know if this was going to work!" he admits.

"The genius of David Kemper is that he keeps changing the rules,"

Andrew Prowse continues. "Think about the story: Crichton gets turned into a statue. He's going to have his head cut off, and dropped into an acid bath… It sounds ludicrous. David's genius is to take these outrageous concepts and make them work. The challenge isn't just one that he takes on, it's one that's passed on to the cast and the director. Sometimes you read a script the first time and wonder what's he doing. He's pushing every boundary in himself at the same time as he's asking you to meet an incredible challenge.

"It was the middle of the season," Prowse adds. "I was doing post-production and visual effects on the earlier episodes, and I was really tired. It was incredibly hard work. With the scale of it, we were pushing the boundaries of a schedule to actually shoot it."

Tony Tilse therefore came on board as second unit director, to take some of the pressure off. "There are a few story strands that I covered," Tilse recalls, "and a few periphery scenes that I could help Andrew with. It's mostly his work — he did the post-production and the edit. I was just helping out with the shooting process, because of the sheer size of the production. It was divided up into what was shot where. I got the whole Zhaan and Moya storyline, and I covered the climbing sequences with Aeryn and Dregon." After handling D'Argo's sex

scene in 'Vitas Mortis', Tilse was also responsible for D'Argo and Chiana's inter-ruption by Crichton. "That was an interesting one to pull off because of what we could get away with, and still keep it tasteful," Tilse says.

One of the funniest scenes in the episode sees Aeryn taking the genetic compatibility test with Rygel. "It's a wonderful moment," laughs Claudia Black. "It works on so many levels for me, putting those things in the script: we learned early on, the more you put your hands on the puppets, the more they come to life."

Team Rygel enjoyed it as well. "We had a lot of help from Claudia in terms of planting her lips right on Rygel's," Tim Mieville recalls. "He doesn't have a tongue, by the way. That was all Claudia's work!"

"In terms of dialogue, drama and characterisation, I love the scene between Crichton and D'Argo," David Kemper says. "D'Argo wraps himself in a blanket and basically tells Crichton he probably has to go through with this. Anthony was so good." ■

Opposite page:
Princess Katralla and
Tyno meet in secret.

Above: *Cargn and*
Scorpius come face
to face.

LOOK AT THE PRINCESS PART II: I DO, I THINK

Written by: David Kemper

Directed by: Andrew Prowse & Tony Tilse

Guest cast: Wayne Pygram (Scorpius), Felicity Price (Princess Katralla), Bianca Chiminello (Jena), Matt Day (Tyno), Tina Bursill (Novia), Felix Williamson (Clavor), Aaron Cash (Dregon), Thomas Holesgrove (Cargn), Francesca Buller (ro-NA), Jonathan Hardy (Kahaynu)

hwarting an assassination attempt on Crichton, Jena, Prince Clavor's fiancée, reveals herself to be a Peacekeeper agent and saves his life. Crichton confronts Prince Clavor, but when his accusations are brought to the attention of the royal family they are dismissed. Empress Novia even starts to have doubts about Crichton's suitability as a match for her daughter. Meanwhile Moya, having followed a mysterious signal, is boarded by Kahaynu, one of her Builders. Zhaan is told, to her horror, that Moya is to be decommissioned because she gave birth to a gunship. As Crichton and Katralla discuss events on the planet, an attempt is made on their lives. To force the conspirators to show their hand, Rygel persuades the Empress Novia to hide Crichton in a place known only to him, the Empress and her most trusted servant, ro-NA. But ro-NA is in league with Scorpius…

> **Zhaan to Kahaynu**
>
> "You must be one of the ship's Builders. One of those who gave Leviathans intelligence?"
>
> "Anybody can give a machine intelligence. We gave her a soul."

For director Andrew Prowse, the fight scene aboard the Jakench ship was one of the highlights of the three-parter. "Crichton's up there and goes crazy. He goes, 'Kill my sex life!', and doesn't care if he gets shot or not. I think it's one of those rare occasions when everything works for you. Ben's performance was great, all the pyros went off beautifully and the music is gorgeous. Ben and I looked at that afterwards and he said, 'There's our show reel!'"

Ben Browder relished shooting the scene, not least because his opponent was his wife, Francesca Buller, returning to *Farscape* after her début as

ENCOUNTERS: JAKENCH

A race of naturally submissive and timid, small green-freckled creatures, whose culture frowns on acquisition. They live to serve, not to possess, and as such can become life-long loyal and trusted servants. However, as ro-NA's betrayal shows, there's always an exception to the rule.

M'Lee in 'Bone to Be Wild'. At one stage Creature Shop supervisor Dave Elsey was going to play the part of the treacherous ro-NA. However, his other commitments meant that he couldn't be in two places at once, so Buller was offered the role. "She was a cool character to play," she recalls. "The moment in the ship when everything was exploding was really amazing. It was quite something to be on a set where if you go the wrong way, you're going to be in trouble. It's like a dance: everybody knows exactly where they're going."

Francesca based her voice for the character on an old BBC recording of Beatrix Potter's *Tale of Mrs Tiggy-winkle*, but the children's author would never have written the scene in which ro-NA battles Crichton. Ben Browder wasn't sure about his wife doing the stunt. "It required me to lift ro-NA up and throw her over my head. I thought, 'Can I raise my hand to the mother of my children?' But she went for it, and came screaming at me with her hands out. I had to pick her up and throw her end-over-end, and pray that she hit the crash mat, because if she doesn't hit the mat, I'm a dead man by the time I get home!"

At the end of the episode, Crichton is turned into a statue — which required Ben Browder to undergo yet another session at Dave Elsey's hands.

Above: The treacherous ro-NA.

Next page: John Crichton and Princess Katralla — united as statues.

"We had already taken casts of every single part of Ben's body," Elsey says, "but we had to take casts all over again for those statues, as well as casts of Felicity Price, who played Katralla. We sculpted those up quite early on, and were in the process of moulding them when I walked onto set and noticed that they had completely changed Katralla's hairstyle. We had sculpted it to match the one that they'd given us originally! We went running back, and luckily we'd only got half the mould on. We had to pull that all apart, completely resculpt the hair in that new style and start again. Those casts were literally finished as we were walking onto set, dabbing them with paint."

Browder had to hold the grimace that he has on the statue while the headcast was taken: "I sucked the material in so it would get around my teeth as well, and hoped it'd come out. If it didn't then they just would've taken a few teeth with it! The hard part was holding the arm position. The head cast was cool. It took fifteen minutes, and the only thing you can do is breathe through your nose. You can't hear. Your mouth is sealed up. You can't see. For fifteen minutes nobody could ask me or tell me to do anything!" ∎

LOOK AT THE PRINCESS PART III: THE MALTESE CRICHTON

Written by: David Kemper
Directed by: Andrew Prowse & Tony Tilse

Guest cast: Wayne Pygram (Scorpius), Felicity Price (Princess Katralla), Bianca Chiminello (Jena), Matt Day (Tyno), Tina Bursill (Novia), Felix Williamson (Clavor), Aaron Cash (Dregon), Gavin Robins (Cargn), Jonathan Hardy (Kahaynu)

ollowing Crichton and Katralla's transformation into statues for eighty cycles, D'Argo and Chiana visit to say goodbye. After they leave, Clavor and Cargn enter and the Scarran chops Crichton's head off, taking it away and throwing it into foundry acid. Empress Novia is outraged at the desecration, and declares a state of "stringent law". As Aeryn is missing (she has gone rock-climbing in the outlands with her would-be suitor Dregon, without telling anyone), she is the prime suspect. Scorpius succeeds in finding Crichton's head, but his imminent departure with his prize is curtailed by Jena. The Peacekeeper agent then revitalises Crichton, and takes him away for interrogation. On board Moya, Zhaan is comforting Pilot as he and the Leviathan die, while in the outlands, Dregon, who is not as experienced a climber as he claimed, falls from the side of a rockface dragging Aeryn with him...

> **Crichton to Scorpius**
>
> " I'm not your enemy. I'm not your friend. You leave me the hell alone. Or the next time we part, one of us'll be dead."

"David Kemper tells me I have a perfect face for radio," Jonathan Hardy jokes. The actor has of course enjoyed a long and varied career on stage and screen, and Andrew Prowse wanted to take advantage of Hardy's experience, bringing him in for an on-screen role as Kahaynu.

"I read the script and then I saw the costume," Hardy recalls. "I swear I looked like Joan Sutherland! The costume designer Terry Ryan and I have known each other since 1421, when I was a boy. The last time he dressed me, I was the Pope in *Pope Joan*. Which was a tremendous performance by the frock... That may have influenced Terry, but by the time he had these huge cuffs on this voluminous costume, it dictated what was going to happen, so I played Kahaynu as Welsh. Then they shaved my hair right back and sprayed on all this make-up. I started to think, 'I don't seem Welsh any more!'

"It was good not having to walk," Hardy adds. "They put me on a trolley!" In the finished episode, Kahaynu appears to be formed from steam. "The idea was to keep him as ethereal as possible," explains Tony Tilse,

who directed Hardy's scenes. "I didn't want him to have too much of a physical form. Jonathan has such a strong presence that I was trying to keep him smoky. It was a consciousness that was travelling through space, which was using gases to form itself. It was tricky to shoot, but fun."

Also tricky to shoot were the rock climbing scenes featuring Aeryn and Dregon, filmed north of Sydney. "Tony Tilse was happy for Aaron Cash and I to do as much as we could," Claudia Black remembers "The silhouetted shot of the stunt doubles and the actual drop were the only things we didn't do. I always hope I'll have enough time to practise, so I can be really proficient at what I'm doing, because Aeryn is supposed to be so proficient. Physically, she's just got to be strong; she should have such a strong presence and be capable."

Ben Browder had some concerns about Crichton's relationship with Peacekeeper agent Jena. "In terms of the character, I felt very dodgy about that," he admits. "I'm surprised that it was as accepted as it was by the fans. Nobody said that I betrayed Aeryn. Somehow we got away with it."

Scorpius's scripted lack of concern after Crichton tries to kill him was emphasised by an idea that came up during filming. "Andrew and Wayne Pygram put in that little bit where Scorpius flicks the acid as he

walks out, and you realise that Scorpius was never really in any danger," David Kemper reveals.

Andrew Prowse has particularly high praise for the final scene. "It pays off the whole opening," he points out. "I was really happy with the whole 'touching tongue' routine. David wrote it initially as kissing, but I thought there was a way of exploring the idea a bit more. Tongue touching is actually sexy, but a bit different. I think that Ben and Claudia did a fabulous job, 'exploring' each other, then Aeryn turns around and gives that little smile. We know that she knows, and then she walks away. Then Crichton knows, but neither of them knows what the other one thought! I loved that."

David Kemper structured the whole trilogy around the first scene and this last one: "They were the only two important scenes. I knew the ending before I thought of another word. If the kiss tastes bad, their relationship is over. I wrote that last scene first — it was just one page, without dialogue. I wrote the whole story to get to that last scene. Andrew, Ben and Claudia had the latitude to make that moment their own and they were spectacular. That scene is the one that lets you know where the series is going." ∎

Opposite page: Aeryn drags Dregon across the outlands.

Above: Cargn realises that Clavor has outlived his usefulness.

MY THREE CRICHTONS

Story by: Gabrielle Stanton & Harry Werksman, Jr.
Teleplay by: Grant McAloon
Directed by: Catherine Millar

Regular cast only

oya is invaded by a small ball of energy which starts to scan the ship and crew one by one. When it approaches Crichton, Aeryn shoots it, but rather than dispersing, it increases its size and engulfs him. After it goes through major energy fluctuations, Crichton is thrown back out of the sphere, followed closely by an ape-like creature, which races away with D'Argo in hot pursuit. Zhaan finds blood on the floor of the maintenance bay, but as Crichton is unhurt, they deduce that it must belong to the creature. However, analysis shows that it is Crichton's blood. Whilst D'Argo searches for the creature, it finds Chiana, and with great difficulty explains to her that it is also John Crichton. Chiana tries to tell the others, but is met with scepticism. While they debate the fate of what they conclude is Crichton's prehistoric clone, the sphere's energy fluctuations recommence and a third Crichton emerges, who is apparently as advanced as the ape-creature is regressed...

> ### Crichton
> " It's bad enough being spat out of some green blob. Now I've got Quasimodo here saying he's me! "

"During season two Ben Browder proved himself to be the Lon Chaney of *Farscape*," says Creature Shop creative supervisor Dave Elsey, fulfilling David Kemper's aim to "put Ben in prosthetics and let him act behind some masks."

"This was the first time that we'd done any make-ups on Ben," Elsey recalls. "We'd always wanted to get him in the make-up chair. I think some of the other actors had wanted to get Ben in the make-up chair just so he knew what they were going through! We were worried about him being the star, and we wanted to make it good. We wanted to make it as comfortable for him as possible, but of course we had to make it *Farscape*, which means pushing it as far as we can."

"Harry and Gaby came up with the really smart idea of not having him be old or young," Kemper explains, "but having Crichton change on the evolutionary scale."

The first alternative Crichton is Neandro, the caveman-like creature. "Neandro was a full fur-suit with a muscle suit underneath," Elsey explains. "It had a chest with bunched hair in it, which Ben was rather fond of. We also had to do his make-up, which was inspired by Dick Smith's work in the film *Altered States*, which is one of my favourite make-

ups. We made the teeth, and wanted to see how far Ben was willing to go. It turned out he was willing to go all the way! He loved wearing the make-up, looked fantastic in it, and worked closely with us. He kept coming in to see how it was progressing, trying things on, and never got bored with helping us as much as possible."

Above: Neandro and Chiana.

Ben Browder had some very clear ideas of how he envisaged the future Crichton, dictating why he chose the Southern accent for Futuro. "If you listen closely, you can actually hear Bill Clinton," he laughs. "In most science fiction, the evolved person is going to be English, and very well spoken. I wanted him to be a big, dark-skinned, bald guy with perfect teeth. But they wanted to make him look alien."

Next page: Zhaan investigates the sphere.

There was a more practical reason behind Browder choosing a different voice: "I looked at the script and realised that if I sounded the same over the comms, talking to myself, it would be confusing as to which one was talking."

"For Futuro, Ben wanted to have these absolutely perfect Hollywood teeth, and he really worked on talking with them," Dave Elsey recalls. "Nobody else was particularly keen on them in production, but I think everybody now agrees that they were a fantastic idea. One of the important things that was stressed to me many times was that they wanted to keep it looking like Ben, and

Ben had to come through the make-up. To be honest, Ben's such a good actor that I think you could have made him up as anything and he still would have come through.

"It was a very complicated episode for us," Elsey adds, "because we also had to have the stuntmen in suits and make-up as well. We realised very early on that we were going to need duplicate versions of everything. You can't do it all with computer graphics: you've got to have stand-ins, people doing stunts and so on."

Claudia Black feels that there were some missed opportunities in the story. "I felt that our characters were dumbed down a little in the process," she says. "Futuro Crichton was the one who was really manipulating the environment, rather than any of us being able to control it. Chiana was the one in that episode who seemed to have the intuitions about Crichton. There was a lot of potential for Aeryn to run through the issues with the various Crichtons, but she never really got the chance."

David Kemper enjoyed the opportunities that were present. "There was some particularly good stuff there because you had Ben playing three roles," he points out. "We had our best gun sitting there, doing multiple tasks in a lot of different scenes. It was a good chance for Ben to flex." ■

| Written by: Naren Shankar | Guest cast: Wayne Pygram (Scorpius), Martin |
| Directed by: Tony Tilse | O'Leary (Ravorc) |

richton is behaving strangely, and Aeryn is worried that he may be suffering from transit madness. Meanwhile, Zhaan and Rygel are discussing the high parasitic content of the system that they are trading in, much to Rygel's alarm and disgust as he inspects food in the cargo bay. D'Argo and Chiana return to Moya with a solution to their problems: a parasite-eating Vorc. Aeryn is unimpressed by the puny creature and wants to jettison the possibly infected food into space. The Vorc urinates on D'Argo then runs away. Crichton discovers a nasty-looking creature in the vents, but when he fires at it, it disappears. The Vorc starts creating chaos, and Zhaan and Chiana try to capture it. Aeryn succeeds in restraining the creature until it bites her and runs off. Crichton sees Scorpius in one of Moya's corridors, but when he goes in pursuit, he only finds Rygel. Just as Aeryn is expressing her displeasure at the Vorc using her quarters as a toilet, "amongst other things", the creature suddenly picks up a scent. Chiana and Rygel come under attack, and D'Argo is seriously injured when he goes to their rescue…

> **Rygel to D'Argo**
>
> "You always expect the worst of me. Is it unthinkable that I might be here simply to offer the gift of my... company to a shipmate in need?"
>
> "Yes."

"There's a very *Lethal Weapon* element to 'Beware of Dog'," reckons Ben Browder. "Ben and I decided we should just focus on Crichton and Aeryn and create some banter," agrees Claudia Black, "since there wasn't really the tension on the ship, or a massive adversity for them."

David Kemper took inspiration from Nicolas Roeg's 1973 film *Don't Look Now* to help set the mood of the piece. "It was the same sort of spooky feeling," he says. "We're haunted — we don't know what it is. It starts off fun, then, in the *Farscape* tradition, it ain't fun…"

However, as Tony Tilse explains, "just through the very machinations of what we had to deal with, it became a romantic comedy." Tilse allowed some

ENCOUNTERS: VORCS

Bipedal predators which hunt and kill a particular type of parasite. They mutate between two forms, one small and built for exceptional speed and tracking, the other larger, stronger and more suitable for combat. Although they do not possess language in a true sense, they can express themselves through a non-verbal mixture of concepts and emotions.

of the horror elements to play through in the final sequence where bugs squirm out of Rygel's eye sockets. "I had just seen the new version of *The Mummy*," he explains. "I loved that moment where the cockroach came out of the Mummy's skin and crawled through the hole in his cheek. I said, 'Wouldn't it be great if we could do something like that? What if Rygel was made out of bugs?'" By judicious use of sultanas with miniature legs glued on them to represent the dead bugs, Tilse freed up the budget to get the shot he wanted. "That's the joy of *Farscape*," he enthuses. "Lateral thinking led to that moment when Rygel's eye popped out."

The humour was also balanced with the appearance of the Scorpius clone in the final scene, although originally he appeared earlier in the episode. "I questioned that," Ben Browder remembers. "I said, 'It's the right scene, but it feels like it's in the wrong place.' We talked about it with the writers, and moved it to the tag so the chess game bracketed the piece."

Although Crichton had hallucinated Scorpius in the hallways during 'Crackers Don't Matter', writer Justin Monjo had intended that as simply a manifestation of the insanity caused by Traltixx. David Kemper realised that it was, in fact, a good way of making use of his main villain. "We have this tremendous character here, and I can't use him," he recalls thinking. "You can't just

have Scorpius come in and not make a big impact; if that happens, he becomes a villain with no balls. So how could I get Scorpius into the show? This thing with him in the hallway worked so well, but that was just part of Crichton's delirium."

Thinking back to the end of season one gave Kemper his answer. "When Crichton was in the Aurora Chair and Scorpius was testing him, he put something in John's head. The audience thinks Crichton got away scot free, but actually, he's got something in his head and he's slowly going to go mad. The chip is going to take over Crichton, and at the end of the year we're going to have to deal with it. At that stage we didn't have a clue why or how, but we knew that during the year we could now have Scorpius coming out to have conversations with Crichton."

Ben Browder believes that this adds depth to the episode. "You have what is essentially a bug hunt on the ship, and the Scorpy stuff gives it a serious moment," he says. "The Scorpy-Crichton relationship is the grounding. There's actually a serious line, which we come back to in the tag, that Crichton is seeing Scorpius and he isn't going to go away…" ■

Opposite page: A game of chess between deadly enemies.

Above: Aeryn cradles the dying Vorc.

WON'T GET FOOLED AGAIN

Written by: Richard Manning	Guest cast: Kent McCord (Jack Crichton), Carmen Duncan
Directed by: Rowan Woods	(Leslie Crichton), Wayne Pygram (Scorpius), Lani Tupu
	(Crais), Murray Bartlett (DK), Thomas Holesgrove (Grath)

During an experimental mission in Earth's orbit, Commander John Crichton's craft, *Farscape 1*, hits an unexpected electromagnetic wave. He faints and the module crashes to Earth. Crichton wakes up in hospital, to find everyone concerned about him. But John Crichton is wise to mind games now. He is certain that he is definitely not back on Earth, and that it's not the real DK and his father who are at the hospital. When he discovers that his doctor, Bettina Fairchild, is the spitting image of Aeryn, and the psychiatrist to whom he is assigned is Zhaan, albeit dressed in a severe business suit, he thinks that things can only get better. That is until astronaut Gary Ragel (bearing an uncanny resemblance to D'Argo) takes him to a bar, where he meets Scorpius...

> **D'Argo to Crichton**
>
> "I'm wondering if you would mind participating with me in a little Luxan bonding ritual. Here's the thing, okay? What we need are, my chains, my Qualta Blade, just a little squirt of lutra oil and... ohh! Chiana. She wants to watch."

"I think 'Won't Get Fooled Again' should come with a government health warning because it's such a freaky thing," Rockne S. O'Bannon warns. "Initially the plan was for me to write the Earth episode," David Kemper explains. "That's what I wanted to do. Then Ricky Manning ended up doing the episode, and he did a better job than I think I would have done. He gave it a level of madness that it needed. Then Rowan just pulled out all the stops."

"It often annoys me," director Rowan Woods says, "that people read into that episode a certain flippancy, a certain joke-telling aesthetic which, of course, is running rampant through the story. But it is a very serious, dark, emotional piece at the same time. For Ricky to wrap his jokemeister ways around those sort of themes was really putting it on the line. I tend to want to shake

ENCOUNTERS: SCARRANS

Large bipedal predators with great strength and dog-like heads. Scarrans' bodies produce intense heat (enough to be felt by those in their immediate vicinity) while their skins are extremely tough and impervious to most weapons. The standard Scarran method of interrogation is to break down all mental defences by inducing hallucinations, pushing the captive to the brink of insanity. They can also extract information with a form of heat wave telepathy, which can be used to kill. The Scarran Empire has a hatred for the Peacekeepers.

people up, not just about alien worlds but their own world. I want to make them ask questions about themselves. Ricky's script demanded that the director really go to some funny places, and some dark places as well. If the director didn't do that, it would have been a disservice to a wonderful piece of writing."

The cast are unanimous in their praise for the episode. For Anthony Simcoe, it was a "chance to break out of how I've defined D'Argo as a character. We take the work seriously, we take the storytelling seriously, but we're always poking fun at ourselves."

"We knew when we were shooting it, that it was good," Ben Browder adds. "Ricky was walking along the parking lot, and I literally prostrated myself in front of him and said it was a beautiful script. With a director like Rowan who you trust, you can do the most outrageous, stupid things and know that he's going to make it work."

"There is a very perverse sexual undertone, which becomes a lot more apparent in the Freudian slip scene with Crichton and his mother," Claudia Black comments. "That's the scene which disturbs most people," Browder agrees. "It does touch a nerve with the audience, and from that point on the Scarran has won. We don't know that it's a Scarran yet, but we just know that this happy jaunt that we're on took a really serious turn."

Above: D. Logan, Dr Kaminsky, DK, Jack Crichton and Dr Bettina Fairchild.

Next page: The coolest drummer in the universe.

The episode contains numerous references back to the first season's 'A Human Reaction', with Crichton checking the ladies' restroom, which didn't exist in the earlier hallucination. It also moves the second season towards its climax, as the Scorpius clone reveals that his mission is partly to protect Crichton. "It's good at that point in the story, and at that point in the season, to tell the audience what's going on, and now they have a context," Ben Browder explains. "This plays for the rest of the season. John is going bonkers: why?"

Amongst the visual highlights of the episode is Lani Tupu in red high heels, carrying a small dog. "I put the heels on, tottered around and fell against the car twice," he recalls of the filming at the Olympic stadium. "We had no idea of the impact of that image, until one of the extras walked around the back of the car, saw me, cracked up and fell about laughing."

Gigi Edgley sums up the feelings of everyone who worked on the episode: "The writer was really pushing it, and some colours came out from every cast member that never existed before." ■

Written by: Justin Monjo	Guest cast: Wayne Pygram (Scorpius), Paul Goddard
Directed by: Ian Watson	(Stark), Allyson Standen (Ennixx)

oya is suspended in space in a fluorescent stellar mist, awaiting the return of Aeryn, who has gone scouting in a transport pod. Meanwhile the Banik Stark has returned to Moya, and joins the crew as they debate their next move. A signal is received from Aeryn, and the pod returns, looking as if it's been in a battle. However, when they board, the crew find that time has been the only aggressor: Aeryn is now an old woman. Although she's only been away for one solar day, for Aeryn 165 cycles have passed, and she has memories of a family. After saying goodbye to Pilot, Aeryn jumps ship, and Crichton follows her down to the planet that has been revealed through the mist. On the planet's barren surface, he discovers that Aeryn has been telling the truth when he meets her grand-daughter. Aeryn convinces Crichton that he must leave or he will be trapped, as the opening in the mist only occurs once every fifty-five cycles in the planet's time frame. But before he can do so, the opening collapses and he too is trapped in another dimension...

> ## Crichton
>
> " Aeryn. You are the one thing which has kept me from doing a kamikaze in the transport. I just have to try to get back to my old life, just for a day. That's the hope. Hope, that's what keeps me goin'."

"Justin wanted to do a love story about people getting old," David Kemper explains. "I thought, let's tell a story where our people go into a cloud and they get old. When they come out, everyone says it was the cloud that caused it, but we discover that it's everyone else who has been screwed up."

'The Locket' was the second unusual season two episode in a row. This was a deliberate move on Kemper's part. "I really liked the idea of following one lunatic episode with a whole other abnormal episode. It was a completely different take on things."

Director Ian Watson loved "the old fashioned, almost creaky quality of melodrama" the episode offered. "It was a clever way of telling a love story, and a wonderful way of building Crichton's and Aeryn's love without having them commit to it. It was a tremendous way of playing out their love on a big canvas without saying it's real. Ben and Claudia loved doing the episode, and they were committed to really making it work well. I felt it would be nice to concentrate on Crichton and Aeryn and their long journey. It was really nice working with Ben and Claudia that closely on something they cared so deeply about."

Dave Elsey and his crew had their work cut out to make the two stars

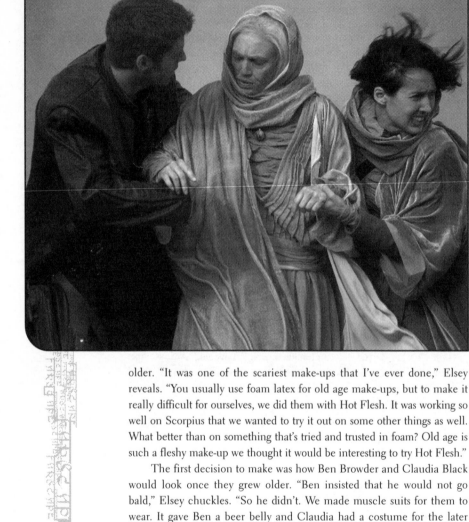

older. "It was one of the scariest make-ups that I've ever done," Elsey reveals. "You usually use foam latex for old age make-ups, but to make it really difficult for ourselves, we did them with Hot Flesh. It was working so well on Scorpius that we wanted to try it out on some other things as well. What better than on something that's tried and trusted in foam? Old age is such a fleshy make-up we thought it would be interesting to try Hot Flesh."

The first decision to make was how Ben Browder and Claudia Black would look once they grew older. "Ben insisted that he would not go bald," Elsey chuckles. "So he didn't. We made muscle suits for them to wear. It gave Ben a beer belly and Claudia had a costume for the later stages of her old age where she had filled out in the hips."

As soon as he got into the make-up chair, Browder started to act as if he was already old. "He was hilarious — as soon as we started he never ever came out of character," Elsey adds. "If we could have got him to sit still as well, it would have been even more brilliant…"

"It was only when I was in the chair with the make-up on that I knew how I was going to do old John," Browder admits. "He develops and

becomes a dumpy, grumpy, lecherous old man. I remember thinking, 'If this make-up doesn't come off, I guess I'm done for. I'll be doing all the fat old characters!'"

Claudia Black also took some of her performance from the prosthetic. "You need to see what you've been given for free and slot in your perform-ance accordingly," she says. "You draw on your whole toolkit of experience as you walk onto set. I brought her voice down a couple of notches, and took out some of the strength that's normally present in Aeryn's delivery. I thought about some little gestures that my great aunt had. The way she sits may not be picked up by the audience as a symbol of old age, but it was something that keyed me into playing her. She was like Katharine Hepburn from *On Golden Pond*: a woman who was rather regal, and not dotty."

'The Locket' also saw the return of Stark. "He was supposed to be a character that appeared in just two episodes in the first season," Paul Goddard recalls, "but then they started talking about bringing him back in some way. I knew that Stark would end up trapped on board Moya for a great period of time." ∎

Opposite page: Crichton and Ennixx help Aeryn through the winds.

Above: Crichton and Aeryn discuss the hidden contents of the locket.

THE UGLY TRUTH

Written by: Gabrielle Stanton & Harry Werksman, Jr. Directed by: Tony Tilse	Guest cast: Paul Goddard (Stark), Lani Tupu (Crais), Peter Carroll (Gahv), Linda Cropper (Fento)

oya meets with Talyn after Crais calls a truce. Aeryn goes aboard Talyn, unarmed and alone, at Crais's request. Chiana and Rygel stay aboard Moya while the others, including Stark, attend a meeting called by Crais. He claims that Talyn is becoming more aggressive and he needs their help to control him. However, during their discussion, a Plokavian ship appears, and Chiana and Rygel watch Talyn's weapons engage and destroy it. Talyn StarBursts away as another Plokavian ship arrives. When the crew try to return to Moya, their transport pod is captured and everyone knocked unconscious before they can reach the safety of the ship. They awaken in an isolation chamber on the Plokavian vessel to find Aeryn missing. She is being interrogated by the Plokavians, who want to identify the person responsible for the destruction of their sister ship. The guilty party will be dispersed. As the suspects are interrogated in turn, each of their five perspectives throws a very different light on the events...

> **Crichton to Aeryn**
>
> " This is the weirdest hoosegow I've ever been in. Slammer, clink, jail, prison."
>
> " Just how many of them have you been in? "
>
> " Just what are you implying? "

"We needed to do a show that was very contained. This was our attempt to do a *Rashomon*," says David Kemper, referring to the famous Japanese film in which the same events are replayed from the different characters' view points. "We could explain a lot about Talyn and Crais, and show Stark as someone who would literally take a bullet for the crew."

Production designer Tim Ferrier's incredible set design meant that the actors were thirty feet above the stage for most of the shots. The water underneath allowed director Tony Tilse to make full use of reflections.

THE PLOKAVIANS

A race responsible for building powerful and dangerous weapons, including Novatrin gas, one of the six forbidden cargoes no Leviathan may carry. Their weapons have helped enslave many planets, including Stark's homeworld. Plokavians, whose features are covered in running sores and sagging skin, need a large amount of dampness in the atmosphere to survive.

"I've always been a mad fan of the director Russell Mulcahy," he says. "There was an old Tubes video he did, which was set over water." Claudia Black adds, "it was very difficult to shoot on those sets because of the disc that we ended up on."

The scenes set on board Talyn were problematic for a different reason. "We all went a bit 'troppo' in there," Lani Tupu recalls. "In other words, we had a bit of cabin fever. The lines were all similar, just slightly different. It was a really good test of staying sane."

"After we shot the different versions, I couldn't remember which was the 'real' one," Paul Goddard says. "We ended up having Crichton's version as the objective reality, but that could be an interpretation as well."

"With everyone's story, you get a hint of what they think of each other," Tony Tilse adds, "and how everyone felt that Crichton was on their side. He agreed with their decisions most of the time. They didn't look like idiots in their own story. Zhaan was such a terrible liar!"

The design for the Plokavians tested Dave Elsey's powers of justification. "The director said he wanted to have two alien characters who were basically melting," he says. "I was trying to talk him out of it. If they were a race that were melting, how long were they going to last? I always

Above: D'Argo, Zhaan, Stark and Aeryn await the Plokavians' judgement.

Next page: The decaying form of Gahv.

try to find a reason for the aliens to be the way they are." However, Elsey went ahead, and took inspiration from "one of the most hysterical films I've ever seen in my life: *The Incredible Melting Man*. Although I'm a great admirer of Rick Baker [that film's make-up artist], I wanted to do something that *wasn't* like that. We designed these heads with goo that would dribble all the time. Tony loved the goo so much that he wanted lots of shots of it dribbling on the floor, hitting the water or dripping off their noses!"

The Plokavians' hoods were costume designer Terry Ryan's responsibility. "They were made out of some sort of packing material," he explains. "When they make rubber, it comes out rough so they slice the top off quite thinly, and it's quite textured. When they pack it to send overseas, they use that outside skin to pack the rolls. We used that. It was perforated, so you could get light through it."

'The Ugly Truth' was designed to be a simple show "that wouldn't kill us, production-wise," David Kemper says. "It had the right genesis, but it just got carried away. Everyone tried to outdo themselves. But that's why *Farscape* is good. You end up with stuff you don't see on other shows. No one takes the easy way out." ■

A CLOCKWORK NEBARI

Written by: Lily Taylor	Guest cast: Lani Tupu (Crais), Wayne Pygram (Scorpius),
Directed by: Rowan Woods	Skye Wansey (Varla), Simon Bossell (Nerri), Malcolm Kennard (Meelak)

Crichton and Chiana return from a scouting trip, during which Chiana has got her shipmates into a fight. Crichton predicts that Aeryn will be furious with her, but when she and Rygel return to Moya, they act in an uncharacteristically pleasant manner. The Nebari Varla follows them on board, and it becomes clear that Aeryn and Rygel have been the subject of drug-induced mind-cleansing by the Nebari, who have come to return Chiana to Nebari Prime. Placing the uncleansed crew in cells, and fitting a control collar on Pilot, Varla forces Moya to head for the nearest Nebari outpost. Although Chiana claims to be in the dark as to why she is so important, Crichton deduces that it has something to do with her dead brother Nerri. Chiana finally reveals to Crichton that she and Nerri had been allowed to escape from Nebari Prime as part of a masterplan by her race to infect the galaxy...

> **Crichton to Rygel**
>
> "You, me and Pilot are the only ones who aren't Nebari puppets."
>
> "I'm nobody's puppet!"

'A Clockwork Nebari' was story editor Lily Taylor's first script for *Farscape*. "She wanted to do a Chiana episode," David Kemper says, "and Lil had the idea to bring back the Nebari. We explained a lot about Chiana and her backstory, and we set in motion the future story for her. Now you know she has a brother out there alive in the underground, which leaves us with great possibilities."

"Up until now Chiana has been searching for her reason for being," Rockne S. O'Bannon notes, "and this gave her a potential quest as well."

Director Rowan Woods is full of praise for the episode. "It was a really beautiful, solid backstory episode, but a tricky one," he says. "It presented this other side of Chiana and the Nebari that we didn't know about. The script was ambitious. It represented the Nebari as a race which not only wipes out others, but dances on their graves! It had an outrageous ending, which involved video trickery, so what I did was head towards that ending and see if I could straddle two different kinds of tones. There was the scary, realistic horror of the Nebari, and something more glib about the way that Crichton deals with the situation and ultimately deals with the ending. I was juxtaposing comedic and horrific scenes, from 'punch the puppet' to someone being tortured, with their eyes pulled out of their sockets. There was a brilliant balancing act in that script, and I had to do it justice."

Gigi Edgley found her role in 'A Clockwork Nebari' very demanding. "I think the ideas were so powerful, and there were lots of emotions coming through on it," she recalls. "You don't often get an episode related wholly to your character, and when they do come along you want to put so much into it. You really want it to go nicely, and explain a lot of your actions in past and future episodes." One of the most gruelling scenes took seven hours to film. "When Chiana freaks out, I really did freak out for them, so by the end, I was absolutely exhausted," Gigi recalls. "The big fight scene took three days to shoot, and by the end of it my body was so stiff it was unbelievable. Character-wise, I had lots of fun with Nerri. It's a shame we only got that one scene together. It was really great to work with Simon. There was some confusion about whether his accent should be Australian or American. The other two were Australian, but they kept

Nerri as American so we knew who the unbrainwashed ones were."

Both Woods and Ben Browder were concerned about the energy level of the episode. Virtually everyone had been mindcleansed, so were reacting in a very laid-back way. "Chiana's the only one who is not brainwashed, or pretending to be, and she's chained up and unable to move," Browder points out. "She also has a heavy emotional storyline. Everybody else on the ship is really happy, and the Nebari are slow, softly-spoken people. I was trying to find a way to do the vacuous brainwashed technique without slowing things down." Thus was born the cool surfer dude. "I'm afraid I have to cop to that," Browder admits. "The interesting thing about that is we have a reference point and a context for what Crichton is saying. The aliens don't know the context, so how are they going to know what Crichton's actual response to the mindcleansing would be?" ■

Opposite page: Varla *tortures Chiana.*

Above: Meelak *prepares Crichton for mind cleansing.*

LIARS, GUNS AND MONEY PART I: A NOT SO SIMPLE PLAN

Written by: Grant McAloon	Guest cast: Paul Goddard (Stark), Wayne Pygram
Directed by: Andrew Prowse	(Scorpius), Claudia Karvan (Natira), Nicholas Hope
	(Akkor), Matt Newton (Jothee), David Franklin (Lt Braca),
	Adrian Brown (Gan), Jennifer Fisher (PK Nurse)

Zhaan insists that Moya follows a course given to her in a vision by the supposedly dead Stark. The others are doubtful, until Stark appears to all of them just as Moya locates a ship with one faint life sign. When they bring Stark aboard, he claims to have a plan to save Jothee: rob a Shadow Depository to get the funds to buy D'Argo's son from the slave auction he is being sold at. Even though Stark has keys and blueprints for the heavily armed Depository, the majority agree that it would be a suicidal mission. Knowing this could be the only chance he has of gaining the money in time for the auction, D'Argo calls the others cowards, and storms off Moya in a transport pod. Crichton and Aeryn follow him in the Prowler down to the rain-swept planet below. While they approach the Depository's custodians posing as potential customers, D'Argo attempts to enter the vault, and is arrested and taken for interrogation by the facility's supervisor, Natira. Enraged, Crichton and Aeryn return to Moya and confront Stark, who reveals that this was all part of his plan...

> **Natira**
>
> "As a race, Luxans can be inartful at love, inadequate at war and intrinsically inept. But this one is intelligent."

"At the beginning of the year I said we were going to rob a bank and blow it up," David Kemper explains. "We knew the first and the third parts were going to be in the bank. The first one was based on *Mission: Impossible*, the second *The Dirty Dozen* or *The Seven Samurai*. The third was *The Guns of Navarone*. That was our template."

"The question came up of what we wanted to do," line producer Anthony Winley adds. "The scope was outside how we originally focused the season. We could have made the episodes very well for the budget, but we wanted to make them bigger and better. The Jim Henson Company advanced us the money — and hopefully it shows." The former president of Henson Television, Rod Perth, even made a small cameo appearance in the first episode.

Tim Ferrier's sets for the Depository filled two entire sound stages at Homebush Bay. "No one, including Tony Winley who produced [the blockbuster sci-fi movie] *Pitch Black*, has ever been on sets that were bigger," David Kemper says in awe. "Timmy built the depositing room, the hallways, the rooms and the windows from nothing, just the genius in his brain."

Above: 'Orala' negotiates with Natira.

"That one goes along like a rocket," director Andrew Prowse says. "It was at the end of the season and we'd got the whole CG process under control. We were doing some really good work. I loved the TV monitors. I think it's got a good rhythm — it's a little rollercoaster."

Virginia Hey relished the opportunity to dress up in a slinky black leather outfit as a piratical villainess. "It was really nice to get into something skin-tight, if only just to feel svelte," she says. "Anything that's dark makes you look thinner. Anything that's pale makes you look bigger. Living for years in pale blue always made me look bigger than I was!"

Mat McCoy, who operates the Rygel puppet, had a scary moment during the scene in which Rygel is inside the money container. "I overbalanced with the puppet," he recalls. "I had Rygel on my right arm, and my left hand was in the Rygel hand glove, so I didn't have any hands, and I overbalanced. The only thing that stopped me from falling a storey and a half was my head. I had to smash it into the wall to try to brace my back and use the force of my head pushing back on the megadeck to stay in place."

One of the most powerful scenes involved Crichton refusing to change Scorpius's cooling rod. "I must have been very tired that day, and I had an idea," Ben Browder recalls. "Instead of saying, 'Get out of my head, Scorpy', I'll sing

Next page: Depository supervisor Natira.

to him, I thought. I'll bellow the national anthem at the top of my lungs. What director in his right mind is going to let an actor bellow the national anthem of the United States of America at the top of his lungs at the pinnacle of the drama? That's insane. You don't do that! It defies all reason, logic and rules of television and film. Yet at the same time it's really quite interesting. Crichton has to have something to fight Scorpy with. I went right back to the potent memories that most Americans who play sports have growing up. There's something about 'The Star-Spangled Banner' that resonates with the kind of guy that John is. Here's your all-American boy, two years later, after being clean-faced and innocent and wide-eyed, screaming 'You're not my type', crawling across the floor, screeching the national anthem!" ■

LIARS, GUNS AND MONEY PART II: WITH FRIENDS LIKE THESE...

Written by: Naren Shankar **Directed by:** Catherine Millar	**Guest cast:** Paul Goddard (Stark), Wayne Pygram (Scorpius), Claudia Karvan (Natira), Nicholas Hope (Akkor), Matt Newton (Jothee), David Franklin (Lt Braca), Thomas Holesgrove (Teurac), John Adam (Bekhesh), Jeremy Sims (Rorf), Jo Kerrigan (Rorg), David Wheeler (Durka), Lionel Haft (Zelkin), David Bowers (Kurz)

The crew realise they will have to buy all the slaves at the auction, rather than just Jothee. However, when they reach the Katin mines, the slaver reveals that they have been prematurely sold in a private deal. He then plays a recording left by Scorpius for Crichton: "John. As recordings are so sadly impersonal, I'll have to imagine what your face looks like now. Etched with failure, I expect. I have Ka D'Argo's son. Surrender to me, or the boy dies." Furious, D'Argo blames Crichton for his inaction earlier, and returns to his quarters where he starts hallucinating about Jothee. When Chiana tries to comfort him, he admits that he had wanted to exchange Crichton for his son. While Aeryn and Pilot investigate mysterious signs of corrosion aboard Moya — which will have shocking consequences for the Leviathan — Crichton outlines his plan to steal the slaves before they reach Scorpius. They will need help from various mercenaries: a Vocarian Blood Tracker, a Sheyang, a Tavlek and a Zenetan pirate...

> **Rygel to Chiana**
>
> "Every time I think that there's more to you than a pair of pushed up loomas in a corset, you disappoint me."
>
> "From you, I'll take that as a compliment."

"Naren said he wanted to write the middle one, and he did a phenomenal job," David Kemper says. "Catherine Millar came in as director and Naren's script gave us great character work, and a real build to the end."

"This is the one where we had to recreate all of the characters that we'd seen in season one," Dave Elsey recalls fondly. "It was so much fun to have everyone on the set at the same time," adds David Kemper.

ENCOUNTERS: KARACK METALLITES

Burrowing creatures which consume metal in their natural environment. They are impervious to anything other than fire and can survive dormant for unspecified lengths of time, in atmosphere or vacuum. In their dormant state, they can be mistaken for pieces of currency.

"The idea was, all of these characters travelled round the universe rampaging, pillaging and stealing things, so when they come up with their costumes, there's bits from elsewhere," Dave Elsey explains. "We decided that we would do a new costume for Teurac. I wanted him to look more like our original designs for the Sheyangs." Six foot two actor Thomas Holesgrove squeezed into the much smaller Sheyang suit. "As soon as you're in that costume, you think that you're small," he comments. "You've got three little stubby fingers. Not being that small, I was really working against it, which felt rather weird."

"As you can tell by the metal thing on his head, Bekhesh isn't too good at ducking when everybody else does," Elsey says of the Tavlek warrior. "We made his armour a little bit more battle scarred than it was before, and added a mechanical implant in the jaw."

Pressure of time meant that Elsey and his team were not able to work as closely on every returning actor as they might have liked. Responsibility for the Vorcarian Blood Trackers was consequently handed over to the make-up department. "In the first season when Rorf and Rorg appeared, they were our very first experiments in Hot Flesh, and they worked out really well," Elsey recalls. "However, because we were now handing them over to the make-up department to handle, we didn't want to give them anything too difficult. We made versions of the Blood Trackers' make-up in foam latex, and they then glued those pieces on."

Both Rygel's voice, Jonathan Hardy, and the head of Team Rygel,

Tim Mieville, enjoyed the scene in which Rygel takes his revenge against Durka. "Rygel's an extraordinary character," Hardy comments. "He's at his best when he's politicking, profiting or dealing as he did with his former torturer!"

Elsey and his team made a cast of David Wheeler's head for Rygel to carry. Elsey found himself explaining to the actor what was about to happen to his character: "'I don't want to give too much away,' I said to David, 'but how would you look if your head was cut off?' He went quiet for a moment then he was fine about it. I didn't think we'd use it half as much as we did," Elsey notes. "It was quite perverse, having Rygel sitting there stroking it!"

The sex scene between Scorpius and Natira was enhanced, following a conversation over dinner between Dave Elsey and Wayne Pygram. "The first time, they shot it like a standard sex scene," Elsey recalls, "and we thought it was far too ordinary. We reckoned Natira should have done something weirder. I thought she should have done something with the spider legs on her head. He should have sucked poison from them, or been strangling her. You shouldn't have known if they were fighting or what. Then we heard they were re-shooting because *everybody* thought it was too ordinary. So Wayne proposed what we'd talked about over our yum cha, and they ended up doing it!" ∎

Opposite page:
Scorpius and
Natira rest after
their exertions.

Above: Jothee held
hostage by Scorpius.

Written by: Justin Monjo **Directed by:** Tony Tilse	**Guest cast:** Paul Goddard (Stark), Wayne Pygram (Scorpius), Lani Tupu (Crais), Claudia Karvan (Natira), Nicholas Hope (Akkor), Matt Newton (Jothee), Thomas Holesgrove (Teurac), John Adam (Bekhesh), Jeremy Sims (Rorf), Lionel Haft (Zelkin), David Bowers (Kurz)

richton, increasingly affected by Scorpius's clone in his brain, has decided to sacrifice himself to the half-breed in return for Jothee. Moya's crew decide that their plan to attack the Depository should stand, except now the object of the rescue will be Crichton. In the midst of a heated debate with the mercenaries, involving much gun-waving, Talyn arrives. While he submits himself to a transfusion to assist Moya's healing process, Aeryn asks Crais and Talyn for help in the attack, but Crais lectures her on the misuse of Talyn's power. While Stark briefs the mercenaries, D'Argo tries to bond with Jothee, but discovers that his son's driving instinct is now self-preservation. Scorpius transports himself inside Crichton's mind, where he declares his intention of killing the human after removing the chip. In a last desperate attempt to obtain Talyn's assistance, Aeryn offers herself to Crais. When the mercenaries raise their doubts about the plan, D'Argo proposes simply storming the Depository. Aeryn interrupts with the declaration that if they can't save Crichton, she will execute him "and end it"…

> **Natira to Crichton**
>
> "Human, you are surprising. I have never seen Scorpius worry about anyone as much as you."
>
> "Don't be jealous, Frau Blücher. He only loves me for my mind."

"The last episode was all about Tony Tilse, or, as I started calling him, Tony Woo," David Kemper says, in a reference to the action-oriented director of *Mission: Impossible 2.* "He was so happy. He had stuntmen

ENCOUNTERS: NATIRA

Blue crustacean biped, with a crown of tendrils which secrete some sort of fluid, and when not folded against her skull can also be used as digits. Although she is Scorpius's lover, she has a maternal instinct toward him, as it was she who took him in when he was abandoned by both the Scarrans and Peacekeepers. Despite this, she also fears and loathes Scorpius, and freely admits that she would attempt to destroy him, if only to earn his respect. Sadistic and self-serving, Natira enjoys torturing and interrogating captives, and has a special fascination for eyes.

on fire, guns going off. He was saying, 'blow that up, blow this up'. I've never seen a man happier!"

"The last two acts were the big rescue, and it was like, 'here we go, guns a-blazing!'" Tilse agrees. "We wanted to make it a big action sequence. I wondered how we were going to achieve battle scene after battle scene. David said, 'We'll do night vision, but Aeryn's won't be working. We'll turn off the lights and just have laser bolts.' And it went from there. We had an infrared camera to do all the night vision. We got into the studio, set up all the pyrotechnics, rehearsed it all, checked all the pyrotechnics — then we turned the lights out in the studio! We shot the scene in the dark, lit by the pyrotechnics going off and using an infrared camera. We've got the best pyrotechnics crew — these guys have done *The Matrix* and all the big movies shot in Australia. They know their stuff. It was spectacular!"

Claudia Black recalls that "it meant you had to have a cast and crew that were ready to work solidly as a team. When you rig up the effects, you don't want to spend another hour setting them up again. The pressure is always on with live effects to get it right the first time. We were told that there was going to be lots of people around us. We were going to be firing, and there were going to be explosions behind us. What we didn't realise — what someone neglected to tell us — was that there would be absolutely no light on the set! The explosions were sufficient to get the shot. They would light up our faces and the

Above: The Zenetans hold Chiana hostage.

Next page: Natira inspects Crichton's eyes.

camera would capture the image. A lot of the extras weren't aware really what it required for us to move through that hallway, so they were all doing very dramatic death scenes and falling at our feet. We were tripping over them, in amidst all these massive explosions."

Those scenes also introduced a new toy for Anthony Simcoe. "My favourite weapon for D'Argo came in season two," he says proudly. "A gun that actually shoots rockets! 'Mr Sparky' is D'Argo's new favourite friend. It's just a great effect because we can get those pyros in shot, really firing."

"David wanted it big, so we gave him *huge*. We thought, 'Let's try and break the record for the number of laser bolts in an episode' — it goes beserk!" Tilse says, also pointing out a typical *Farscape* moment in the midst of the chaos. "There's a guy on fire and Scorpius walks in and ignores him. He's got other things to worry about. It's his obsessed moment."

While all this was going on, the object of the rescue was strapped to a large steel ball. "This was right on the heels of the crucifix, of eye-gouging and every other device that they'd strapped me into during the year," Ben Browder is at pains to point out. "It was very uncomfortable, suspended upside down with a steel bar driving into your spinal column. Next time, the art director gets to spend an equal amount of time in the contraption he designs for the actor!" ∎

DIE ME, DICHOTOMY

Written by: David Kemper	Guest cast: Paul Goddard (Stark), Wayne Pygram
Directed by: Rowan Woods	(Scorpius), Lani Tupu (Crais), Matt Newton (Jothee), David
	Franklin (Lt Braca), Hugh Keays-Byrne (Grunchlk),
	Thomas Holesgrove (Diagnosan Tocot)

rais and Talyn have located a Diagnosan, Tocot, who may be able to heal Moya and remove Scorpius's chip from Crichton's head. Crichton's condition is worsening, to the point of losing his identity to Scorpius's clone. Tocot comes aboard and claims he can help Moya, but his manager, Grunchlk, insists on an exorbitant price. Aeryn discovers Crichton messing with Moya's communications, but he claims that being busy helps keep him under control. Although Crichton then declares his love to Aeryn, it's actually a ploy by Scorpius's clone to manip-ulate her, before smashing her skull against a bulkhead. Crais and Talyn discuss their desire to bring Aeryn aboard, but they are interrupted when Talyn intercepts a Peacekeeper signal known only to captains and above. When Jothee discovers Crichton's treachery, he con-fronts and tries to attack him, but is overpowered by

Crichton to Aeryn

"Ah, did I... say or do any-thing to piss you off? I mean, other than caving in the side of your head?"

Crichton. His gloating is cut short when D'Argo renders him unconscious, and he is taken down to Tocot's surgery. The Diagnosan examines the human's brain but says there is nothing he can do. He cannot remove the neural chip without killing Crichton... ∎

SCRIPT TO SCREEN

" Welcome to our world, baby! "

– John Crichton

David Kemper

"The first third of each year we have stand alone episodes that help keep the story alive. During the second part of the year, the story starts to form, and then in the third part, we pay it off. It's like reading a novel."

"I come up with images that tell stories that work," explains *Farscape*'s executive producer David Kemper. In the case of season two's cliffhanger, 'Die Me, Dichotomy', "I knew the last image was Crichton lying on a table. The only surgeon in the world who could take Crichton's brain out and put it back in was standing there doing an operation and removing Scorpius's chip. Scorpius comes in, kills the surgeon so there's no one else who can heal Crichton, takes the chip and leaves. Crichton is strapped to the table, unable to speak, part of his brain missing and the only person that can heal him is lying on the ground."

To turn that image into reality took hundreds of people. But first, Kemper had to work out the story. "As we were writing 'Liars, Guns and Money', I was trying to think what the obvious ending should be. If the chip is taking over Crichton's personality, it ought to take him over completely, and turn him into Scorpius. I asked Dave Elsey if we could do this and he said, 'Absolutely'. The image of Ben as Scorpius was really important, because it crystallised what I wanted. I also knew there would be a planet with frozen people everywhere. The set guys were conceptualising that early on. You start to piece together things as you go and all of a sudden, when it's time to shoot, all they're missing is the script!"

The cast knew that someone was going to die, but not who. "I didn't know who it was," Kemper admits. "I was doing the outline and had Aeryn in her Prowler chase Crichton in the module through space. Then Ricky Manning said, 'We've done it in space; why don't you do it over the surface of the ice planet?'"

That didn't alter Kemper's fundamental idea for the script. Under the chip's control, Crichton would fly away in the module. Aeryn would chase him, but it would be an uneven contest because "she's a phenomenal fighter pilot and he has a ship with no weaponry. He puts up a good fight, but she's better and shoots him down." Aeryn would feel guilty about causing Crichton to crash, but the surgeon would be able to fix him and remove the chip from his head.

"As I was working on the script," Kemper says, "I remembered Sam Rolfe, one of the creators of *The Man from U.N.C.L.E.*, telling me, 'When a scene doesn't work, flip the motivation.'" If two characters have opposing feelings for each other, then changing the dialogue so each says the other's lines might produce a better dynamic for the scene. "Once in a while, you get a gem out of it," Kemper notes.

So it proved. Kemper asked himself why Aeryn shouldn't be the one to crash on the ice planet, and realised that she could. "Crichton is Scorpius and he's clever," he explains. "She doesn't see that cleverness. She thinks she's chasing Crichton but it's really Scorpius." If she crashed, what would Crichton's reaction be? "That might shock the real Crichton into taking control of Scorpius enough to bring Crichton back," he continues. Crichton could then ask his friends for help, and they could arrange for the surgeon to remove the chip and heal Aeryn…

It was at that moment that Aeryn's fate was sealed. "I thought, why shouldn't Aeryn get killed?" Kemper says. "She can die. Once I knew that Aeryn was dead and I wanted the audience to really believe that, I had to have a funeral that blew people away. I had to go back and start over. I had written half the script. There's thirty pages of 'Die Me, Dichotomy' that nobody will ever see because I threw them out.

"I changed the outline. They were frantic for the script and I was sending it in an act at a time. I sent in act two and Lil Taylor says, 'David, this isn't anything like the outline. Nothing is the same.' 'Oh — did I forget to tell you? I started over.'"

One of the key elements to sell the story was Crichton physically becoming Scorpius (to the viewer at least). "We designed exactly the same make-up as we did on Wayne Pygram," Creature Shop creative supervisor Dave Elsey says, "but we sculpted it on Ben. We'd asked if anybody wanted any changes, and they said, no, it should be exactly like Scorpius, except that we'll know that it's Ben because he's built completely differently to Wayne.

He's physically much bigger, with completely different eyes, and a differently shaped face. So we were not concerned that anyone would ever mix up the two — but then we had the first day of shooting." Ben Browder continues: "They were watching the rushes, and people said, 'These scenes are good, but why is Wayne doing them?'" A quick solution for the confusion was needed. "There was a big crisis discussion about what we should do," Elsey says. "So we decided to remove the teeth, so he had Ben's own teeth, and basically he'd have Ben's colouring."

"I've been watching Wayne for a year and a half," Browder adds. "I tried

to pick out a few signature, hallmark Scorpy things and utilise those. Wayne has a peculiar, unusual phrasing which is particular to Scorpius. He will stop in the middle of a line and then run over the sentence."

'Malibu Scorpius', as he was nicknamed, wasn't the Creature Shop's only work on the episode. "We had to create Grunchlk, for Hugh Keays-Byrne," Elsey says. "He told us how he was going to play it, and we said we had to make him into a grotbag. We wanted to get the teeth really bad because he's forever eating things, and figured he's going to have sores from the dribbling."

Hugh Keays-Byrne was one of the actors who had auditioned for D'Argo at the start of *Farscape* and although he didn't get the role, David Kemper had wanted to include him in the show ever since. "I called him up at his farm in Queensland and we had a long talk," Kemper says. "Originally, Grunchlk was going to die, but we decided not to kill him off. Hugh was too good."

Grunchlk is manager to the Diagnosan, Tocot, whose genesis is described in the Creature Shop chapter. "I think Tocot was one of the better creatures that we did last year, if not the best," praises line producer Anthony Winley, "I liked the whole way that his animatronics worked."

Thomas Holesgrove was approached by Dave Elsey to take the role while playing the Sheyang in 'Liars, Guns and Money'. "He gave me a lot of

Page 79: Ben Browder is transformed into Crichton-Scorpius.

Opposite page: Crichton-Scorpius and Aeryn in the neural cluster.

Above: Putting the finishing touches to Tocot's make-up.

points of reference," the actor recalls. "I looked at a lot of videos of Peter Cushing in the Hammer Frankenstein movies and studied his hand movements — the mad scientist and the way he moves."

Puppeteer Fiona Gentile is heard on the soundtrack of the finished episode providing Tocot's memorably alien voice, though originally she was only going to supply a guide voice on set, during filming. "Fiona came to me and asked what we wanted for the voice," David Kemper says. "Rowan and I decided it would be a woman, just for Ben and Hugh to have something to play off. We talked to her about what was appropriate, and she could have just shown up on set and done it, but she came back two days later to demonstrate it for us. That extra step of dedication, the fact that she had worried about it and worked on it on her own, is the microcosm of *Farscape*. The way we rewarded that was, when we heard it, we let her do the voice you hear in the episode."

The next requirement: Crichton's brain. "We built a brain that would actually fit inside Ben's head," Dave Elsey explains. "It was actual size, then we used a vacuum-formed copy of Ben's head with clear skin over the top. We filmed that separately from Ben, then they combined the two together in post production, and that worked really nicely."

Rowan Woods was selected to direct 'Die Me, Dichotomy', which he describes as the "button-pushing script of all time. I reckon Kemper's greatest virtue is that he's completely unafraid. He's committed to pushing buttons that people don't know they have. The other thing I like about 'Die Me, Dichotomy' is it's so well plotted. I didn't know we could do it until we got

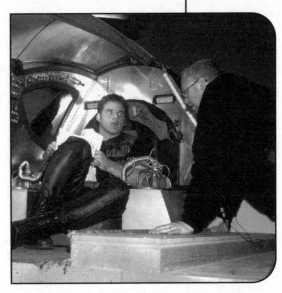

the script! I was a bit nervous about doing the boss's script for the first time. You really have to be careful not to invent too much extraneous stuff. If you go off the tracks, you do it at your own peril. In the four weeks beforehand, I just asked David stupid questions and he'd give me, as he does, hour-long answers. In the process of five or more long conversations, I got two important notes — one of them was that Rygel is a great character." Although the Hynerian is not central to the episode, both Ben Browder and Rowan Woods nominate the haggling between Rygel and Grunchlk as one of their favourite moments. "That's a classic Kemper scene," the director notes. "Even Aeryn Sun seems immature when she comes to interrupt."

One of Claudia Black's less favourite times came during the scene in Moya's neural cluster, when Crichton-Scorpius licks her face. "Those things are hard to perform when you're supposed to be knocked out and not react at all, and he has to go for it," she points out.

The neural cluster also saw the confrontation between Crichton-Scorpius and Jothee. "Matt Newton comes forward and takes the hit, which is just beautifully timed," Ben Browder recalls. "I must have watched the rushes on that thirty times and creased up every time. He was knocked out, and for a second his foot comes up into the bottom of the frame. It was the perfect pratfall." Newton also has happy memories of shooting the scene: "We literally could not stop laughing that day. I'd done three years at drama school, so I'd learned how to do pratfalls and physical stuff like that."

Through all the versions of David Kemper's script, the ice planet and its 'mortuary' of frozen bodies had been a constant element. Production designer Tim Ferrier and his team created sets that "looked like something out of a movie," according to Paul Goddard. "Those sets and designs worked absolutely brilliantly. The way they were built meant that they really came alive. With the ice and the fog, even though it was really bright, it seemed rich."

The ice planet was the setting for the central sequence of the episode: the chase between Crichton-Scorpius and Aeryn. Rowan Woods' second note from David Kemper was that "they won't believe that Aeryn is going to die." Woods therefore directed the episode on a simple basis: "There's always

Opposite page: Tocot and Grunchlk give Crichton the bad news.

Above: Director Rowan Woods discusses the next scene with Ben Browder.

going to be doubt in the audience's mind, but if you can completely commit yourself to the idea that a dear friend, as Aeryn has become, is going to die, then it can be a beautiful moment."

Filming the chase called for careful preparation. "It was so tough in two weeks to do a seven-minute dogfight according to what David had written," Rowan Woods says. "I immediately had to sit down and storyboard it in absolutely meticulous detail with Andrew Prowse, and just tweak until I was satisfied with it."

Much of the sequence was prepared in post-production, but Claudia Black's performance was the central pillar around which it was based. On the day that Black filmed Aeryn's death scene, David Kemper asked Andrew Prowse, who directed the sequence, for a chance to speak to the actress before she was dropped into the water. Forty feet above the studio floor, "there was no railing and it was scary," Kemper says. "I was on a wooden platform. I grabbed onto a wire and leant out over the water. There was Claudia in the chair, in her wetsuit. She had several expressions on her face. One was, I'm about to get wet. Another was, they're about to drop me and it's a terrifying experience. And the third one was an unmistakable, friendly look of murder! I wanted to use that moment to let her know that the executive producer thought that this was one of the finest year-long performances he'd ever seen. This wasn't punishment but a reward: she had earned the storyline she was living through."

"If anything went wrong underwater it would be a couple of seconds at least before anyone could get to me and give me oxygen," Black explains. "I came up with a safety signal. I wanted Aeryn to be shouting Crichton's name

and be interrupted, and taken down before she's ready. I had to also try to count and gauge how many seconds I was under before they'd pull me up. There were cameras filming me underwater, so I couldn't be counting visibly. I had to act underwater, and trust that they would pull me up, get me to a level where I could speak and not be flooded with water, say the line, and then have them pull me down. We worked it through. The stunt people knew what I was doing, so they were able to lower me down before I finished the word.

"They weren't expecting the water to be so murky," she adds. "I quite like it — it's an incredibly dramatic image to see Aeryn descending into something that looks quite uninviting. She starts to break down, and when you see her go underwater you're not sure if she's died or not. Until that final movement of the hand, and you know — that's it." Composer Guy Gross notes that he was specifically asked to "make sure everyone knew that she was dead when her hand fell."

Opposite page: The crew say their farewell to Aeryn.

"I was glad when I read the script that there was a funeral," Claudia Black says. "We all got quite emotional and sentimental in that scene. It was incredibly difficult playing dead because it went on for a very long time. Zhaan was just going on and on, and I'm lying in this coffin with a load of CO_2 smoke, which diminishes the amount of oxygen available to you."

"I wanted to deliver the speech quicker," Virginia Hey points out, "but with all the camera moves and the things that they had to achieve, I had to time it out, and say the lines very slowly. It felt bizarre talking that slowly for the whole speech."

"Rowan directed that really beautifully," Anthony Simcoe notes. "The simple gestures and moments encapsulated everything that needed to be told at that time." These included his character placing his trusty Qualta Blade in the coffin. "It was Rowan's idea," Simcoe adds. "It's a really significant gesture for D'Argo."

"You can't shoot a funeral without paying a deep-seated emotional homage to your own experience," Woods explains. "I realised that these guys would do anything. I love that moment. It's so full of irony too, when Jothee's hand clasps Chiana's in comfort."

Gigi Edgley felt uncomfortable with the increasing intimacy between Chiana and D'Argo's son in the cliffhanger. "That was pretty hard, morally, for me to deal with," she says, "so I really had to throw myself deep into it. I went to David who said, 'We want Chi, not Gi. Let's play.'"

The aftermath of the funeral saw the various characters apparently ready to disperse. "It was a great emotional journey for Crais because his true feelings are revealed," Lani Tupu says of his dialogue with Talyn after Aeryn's death. "The difficult thing was, I was holding this chip, and I had no idea what the reference was to!" Scapers will have to wait until well into the third season to discover the significance of that chip…

"There's a whole load of little closures that very successfully introduce levels of ambiguity and raise questions while maintaining the tension of the moment," Rowan Woods points out. "Did Crichton say yes to Tocot about whether he should cut his memories of Aeryn? There's a lot left unsaid between Grunchlk and Rygel in that moment in the corridor. Is that a marriage proposal from Stark to Zhaan or just a friendship offer? What's going to happen with Chiana and Jothee?"

And, of course, what is going to happen to Crichton? "I got strapped to another device," Ben Browder sighs. "They strapped me to a table again! Then I got to yell gobbledegook — it was the writers' revenge: 'We'll take away his pop culture references. Let's see how he does without any lines at all!'"

Once the actors had finished filming, the episode moved into post-production. For the actors, this involves re-recording their lines in ADR (Additional Dialogue Recording). "It is always hard to get the original qualities in the performance again, and that's what we are fighting for in ADR," Claudia Black comments. "Angus Robertson and I fought to really bring it back."

For Rowan Woods, Andrew Prowse and the visual effects team at Animal Logic, it meant bringing the storyboards of the chase sequence to life. "You strip back the storyboards to what you can afford and try and think of clever ways of making the story work," Prowse explains. "What's absolutely required, and what's not strictly necessary, but will nevertheless be really cool in CG? The computer animators are fanatical about the show. They wanted to do extraordinary things. They wanted to express themselves and I'd be crazy not to let them go with that. A really good

example of that is the shot where Aeryn fires the retrorockets on her ejector seat. One of the animators built a 3D chair, stuck a 3D Aeryn into it, and ripped it up into space."

"It's a one-second shot," Woods expands. "It's like the standard shot you see in skydiving documentaries, which represents gravity in a real, visceral way: when the parachute is released, the skydiver who's being videoed shoots up into the air, above the guy who's videoing it. That shot with Aeryn makes a fantastic, emotional rollercoaster moment just sing in a very realistic sense."

"If I had suggested doing that, it would have cost us another ten to fifteen thousand dollars, but this guy stayed overnight and did it," Andrew Prowse adds. "He was there for thirty-six hours to get this shot! Everyone knows that they're working on a once-in-a-lifetime thing."

Prowse also liaised with supervising sound editor David White and his team. "The temptation was to make the whole sequence get bigger and bigger," White recalls. "Fortunately, Andrew Prowse has a good ear in terms of structuring sound. The whole idea of pulling back on the effects after Aeryn was propelled out of the Prowler, going much more with the music and then going virtually to silence when she drowns, was dramatically far more powerful. It was probably not the way we would have done it had we done it on our own."

Post production supervisor Deborah Peart had to find the footage to represent Crichton's memories. "We had to do a lot of chasing for stock footage for those tiny little sequences we see when Crichton talks about American politics. We had a hard time getting clearances to show it all. Then I had to run around the set and production getting dog photos! David Kemper's dog is in there, and some of the animators over at Animal Logic got their pups in."

As the post production process continued, editor Nicholas Holmes prepared a rough-cut, adding some suitable temporary music, just to help the mood. In this case, Holmes chose 'Nimrod' from Elgar's *Enigma Variations* to accompany Aeryn's death scene before Guy Gross's music was added.

When the final edit was ready, it was sent to the various producers around the world who have to clear each episode of *Farscape*. On 6 October 2000, series creator Rockne S. O'Bannon and David Kemper signed off their copies. "It's really important to make a resonant season ender," O'Bannon comments. "There's a lot of scope to what's going on, but at the centre of it is the emotional tug on several different fronts."

"Our season enders are good because everyone involved is happy," David Kemper concludes. "We try to put some really good, challenging work in front of them so that they are kept interested, and they always respond. Everybody responds. They add levels of quality, class and professionalism that cannot be anticipated by a script." ■

Opposite page:
Afternoon tea at
Homebush Bay
— the cast and
crew take a break.

THE CHARACTERS

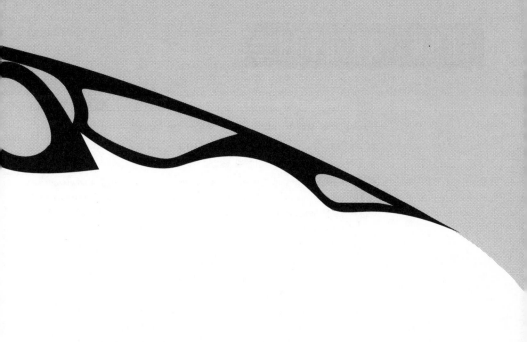

"I've become so distrustful of people, even when they're trying to

help me. What does that say about what I've become?"

- D'Argo

"Does this strike any of you superior beings as a little bit ironic? I'm the deficient one and I'm still saving your butts."

"What Crichton and Aeryn's relationship has at its heart is this guy and this girl in extraordinary circumstances," Ben Browder summarises, looking back at the second season. John Crichton is "slowly unravelling, and he's not sure why. The only person he ever talks to about it is Aeryn. They're comfortable in the beginning of the year, and as the season goes on she becomes his rock. She keeps him centred."

Before the Scorpius chip begins to make itself felt in Crichton's brain, Browder believes that Crichton and Aeryn are "much more alike by the beginning of season two. By the first episode of 'Liars, Guns and Money', you have Crichton hearing Scorpius's voice in his head, and getting ready to learn about the chip. The buzzing in his ear, hearing voices, is starting to become more than a nuisance. It's starting to dictate actions to him. To counteract that, he kisses Aeryn. She is his focus, his way out. I think there's a depth to the relationship that they have which is in some ways beyond lovers, even though they are not lovers. There are circumstances that keep them from being lovers. Yet in many ways they are beyond that point."

While Crichton and Aeryn may not be sexually involved, "they're fully engaged in every other way," Browder says. "They run through the halls in 'Beware of Dog' like an old married couple with a weapon. They actually start to talk in sync. He starts stealing her lines and she starts stealing his — Crichton is becoming more like Aeryn. Then there is a beautiful moment in 'Die Me, Dichotomy' where Aeryn leans in and puts her head on Crichton's shoulder. That is a direct lift of things that John has done on at least two occasions. There's a fascinating kind of crossover there, and the interplay which comes with it is very small, detailed work that most people are not going to notice. There are simple little things that are brought into the performance that Claudia does wonderfully. In the end it makes for a very interesting couple. They have reached a certain place and yet aren't able to make the final step."

This isn't caused by Crichton's feelings for Chiana. "I think Crichton fancies the hell out of Chiana," Browder admits. "He just knows Aeryn would probably kill him so he's not going to do anything about it! He's focused for the most part on Aeryn, but maybe if the circumstances were right with Chiana, there might be something. She's sexy, but she's grey! I'm not sure John is comfortable making the crossover to alien sex; he has a reticence about that. I think that's natural and normal."

By the time the Vorc comes on board, Chiana is with D'Argo and

Crichton is aware that he has a problem of a very different nature — Scorpius's chip. "But he can only talk to Aeryn about it, no one else," Browder points out. "He and Aeryn have so much interaction that it makes the stakes emotionally high. It also gives her and John a reason not to take the next step in their relationship, because she knows he's got a problem. She's keeping his confidence — nobody else knows this is going on."

The problem continues to get worse, as the Scorpius chip starts to bleed through into Crichton's personality. "The later episodes begin to explain a lot of John's behaviour in the early part of the season," Browder says, "which is a wonderful gift by the writing department for me. I'm playing a lead character who is ostensibly going insane. The KFC reference in 'Liars, Guns and Money', when I say, 'It is to my knowledge unique in the universe, and unique is always valuable', is a direct lift from Scorpius, when Scorpius talks to John in 'Look at the Princess'. In 'Beware of Dog', John takes an affinity to the ball that Scorpy likes. By the time he draws a weapon on Stark in 'Liars, Guns and Money' I think it's hard to differentiate which is madness and which is his outlook. Is it the Scorpy chip? Is it John in reaction to the Scorpy chip? A reaction to the universe he's living in? It's really hard to differentiate. There are moments

sometimes when Crichton sees what he's done and doesn't like what he sees in the mirror."

When Crichton hands himself over to Scorpius in exchange for Jothee, Browder believes that the astronaut makes the choice himself. "Scorpius wants to think that it's the clone that's forcing him, but I think John's exhausted his options. If he continues on this path, coming up with violent plans, pulling guns on people, where is it going to end? He can't see an end to it and he's becoming a danger to everybody."

During the season we learn one of Crichton's hidden secrets — his relationship with his mother. "Crichton never mentions his mother," Browder says. "That's deliberate. I think it showed up in one script somewhere in season one and I cut it. I've got a Southern boy thing: your mother is the central thing in your life. John's dad was off being an astronaut, so his mother raised him. We'd talked about the back-story, of Crichton not being there when she died." In 'Won't Get Fooled Again' Carmen Duncan appears as Leslie Crichton, dying of cancer, alongside Kent McCord, returning as Crichton's father Jack. "John's greatest regret and his greatest fear is losing his moth-er, and he wasn't there for her," Browder adds. "It's a huge thing and, out-side of that episode, Crichton has still not talked about his mother. People talk about characters having demons; people also have deep regrets. After forty episodes of *Farscape*, he's still never discussed it. That's what makes the character interesting — it's not just what he'll talk about, it's what he won't talk about."

As an actor, Ben Browder enjoys the challenges that playing John Crichton brings. "People are continually changing, especially John, because of the extraordinary circumstances," he says. "John changes con-stantly. Every now and then, he'll backslide to what he was before, but there's been an evolution of his character that I find fascinating. In most television, there's an attitude of, 'that's who the character is and he's always that.' David Kemper is fond of saying, 'people change.' I'm not sure if that's true in real life or not, but it's definitely true in *Farscape* and it makes it much more interesting. I've been given the option to have the gauntlet thrown at me and slapped in my face by the writing department. I've played an old man, different versions of myself, I've played Rygel inheriting my body. There are actors who go through their entire careers and never have the opportunities that I was given in season two alone." ∎

"I'm just an ignorant warrior who believes that love means you're willing to fight and die for your fellow living beings."

"Creatively, I launched into season two with a more solid foundation," Claudia Black says of former Peacekeeper Aeryn Sun, whose death at the hands of Crichton-Scorpius brings the season to a tragic end. "I felt more confident by the end of season one that I was ready to do what I felt was right. Very early on in season two we had some wonderful character episodes, and that's where I started to get much more enthusiastic. I'm very hard on myself, and I did find it very difficult to break Aeryn out of that two-dimensional Peacekeeper mould."

The increased physical intimacy between Crichton and Aeryn, noticeable at the end of 'Mind the Baby', began that process. "I think it's been clear from the very beginning of *Farscape* what we've been asking the audience to believe in," Black says. "We felt that we had earned the right to have that physical proximity because of what has just happened. It's a turning point. Ben and I could display something deeper in their friendship. They were comfortable with one another in the room. We felt that they had earned that right to be gentle with one another."

Crichton and Aeryn spent the year learning more about each other. "In 'Taking the Stone', they are trying to work as an emotional couple rather than a fighting team," she says. "That is the beginning of a deeper understanding. They should just allow each other to be as they are, rather than mould the other into something they're not.

"'Crackers Don't Matter' inspired me to find new ways to play Aeryn during the season," Black explains. "She could become more normal in other areas, and we could explore parts of her humour and idiosyncratic behaviour."

In a different way, 'The Way We Weren't' was a significant episode for Aeryn. "She quite outwardly sobs," Black recalls. "That's probably the only time we've seen Aeryn do that. On other shows, characters cry at the drop of a hat. We've had to be quite specific about when Aeryn shows that emotion. There's a weight to it when you see her cry, because something is really changing inside of her."

Aeryn doesn't completely lose her Peacekeeper mentality; it's still there when she needs it. In 'Home on the Remains' she knocks Zhaan unconscious, and she doesn't hesitate to slug Crichton when he wants to go to Scorpius in 'Plan B'. "It is her last resort," Black points out, "but when she does it, she's done something major. Although she's learned not to use her weapons or violent actions to resolve things, what I love about Aeryn is that you're reminded every time she does those things of where she came from and who she is."

In 'Look at the Princess', it seems as if Crichton and Aeryn's relationship is at an end when he agrees to marry Princess Katralla. "I think it's important with the ebb and flow of their relationship, that when an adversity comes they take it in turns to fight for the relationship," Black notes. "Crichton changes a lot as they swap their roles. He becomes quite jaded and starts to concede to the environment around him a lot more, rather than fight to change it. The stakes are higher for Aeryn. She refuses to believe that the politics of this situation can be strong enough to dominate a relationship which is more important to her. It's quite a selfish reaction, but it's nice to see her finally start to fight for something, rather than pushing him away."

Aeryn gets some good advice from unlikely sources during the 'Look at the Princess' trilogy, initially from Chiana. "There is quite a lot of antagonism between Aeryn and Chiana, until she and D'Argo become romantically involved," Black says. "When they're sitting by the water and Chiana is giving Aeryn advice about men, there's an understanding between them that Crichton is more important to Aeryn than she will concede."

That advice is reinforced by Dregon. "He has the generosity to offer her some wisdom that night by the fire, and says that Crichton isn't going to know how she feels unless she tells him," Black recalls. "That's a pivotal point for

Aeryn, and it motivates her to move on and show Crichton how she feels. The scene at the end, when Aeryn offers Crichton the vial, was the most exciting tag we had read to that point. It's the longest non-speaking scene we'd had. It's hard to convince people that the characters and actors can play scenes without words, and the characters had definitely earned the right to do it all with their eyes."

In 'Beware of Dog', Crichton sees another side of Aeryn, as the Vorc dies in her arms. "Surprisingly, we get some emotion out of Aeryn," Black says. "I think it's important for Crichton to witness Aeryn having empathy with something that she's been quite aggressive towards."

Before Scorpius's chip starts to take control of Crichton, changing his personality dramatically, he and Aeryn share a long life together in 'The Locket'. Black is glad that neither character remembers that afterwards. "To bring that knowledge back up to Moya would be a dangerous thing," she says. "But it's nice that they have a sense that something has passed between them. It's like one of those classic romantic relationships in movies, where you know that the characters aren't necessarily suited to one another, but they are inexorably drawn together."

During the 'Liars, Guns and Money' trilogy, Black was careful to ensure that Aeryn's reactions to Crichton's increasing madness were true to the character. "I had to track her level of concern," she says. "How seriously is she taking his madness? Is it just 'Erp Boy' being stupid again, just being human? I think, because of the way that Aeryn feels about Crichton, she puts a lot of it down to him being from a planet called 'Erp'."

When Crichton hands himself to Scorpius in exchange for Jothee at the end of 'With Friends Like These...', Black "knew where my character's heart was," she explains. "For me, the choice has become easier and easier for Aeryn to be vulnerable. She couldn't be in the beginning, but now she's starting to release."

Aeryn finally declares her love for Crichton in 'Die Me, Dichotomy', unfortunately, after the Scorpius clone has taken full control. Black believes that Aeryn pays the ultimate price for her increasing vulnerability when Crichton-Scorpius brings the module down into her Prowler cockpit: "Crais says, 'Don't trust him', but I don't think in her heart Aeryn wants to believe that Crichton would pull a stunt like that. There's a duality in her that makes it so hard for her to control herself. I love the moment when she's going down in the chair and she says, 'I hope you meant what you said in the neural cluster, I did'. Down she goes — she's so vulnerable." ∎

KA D'ARGO

D'Argo

"My life has been one crushing disappointment after the next but with this girl, I have managed to find moments of pleasure."

"It was lovely to see D'Argo talk about a relationship all the time," considers Anthony Simcoe, who had a more comfortable year in the Luxan's tentacles after the streamlining of his make-up at the beginning of the season.

Simcoe has "never worked on any other television show or film where the actors are completely trusted. If we feel that a moment isn't working, we change it. Some of the best moments come out of those decisions." Certainly, through the year he and Gigi Edgley spent a lot of time discussing how they should play the relationship between D'Argo and Chiana.

"We were really excited about it," Simcoe remembers. "Gigi and I have a really great working relationship. It helps settle Chiana into the show for us to be working together all the time. It's Gigi's first long-term gig, so it served that practical function. Gigi also brings out fantastic things in me and I think we really complement each other as actors. We approach work very differently and we appreciate that in each other. I think it serviced the characters tremendously, because it gave us the opportunity to bring out other dimensions in both of them."

Simcoe thinks that the Luxan warrior used to be a "planet slut" — D'Argo would go down to planets, find a girl, have a brief relationship, then return to Moya. In comparison, "it was nice to see how D'Argo interacts with people intimately in those kind of moments. It was good to flesh that out."

The actor isn't surprised that fans found it difficult to accept the relationship. "I don't think the audience did buy it right from the start, but in a good sense," he qualifies, "in the sense that they picked up that it wasn't going to last. It was a doomed relationship right from the start, and picking up on the sense that it's doomed is what creates the tension, so that's not a failing in any sense. These people aren't really matched. There's some need in them that is being fulfilled for the moment, but if the stakes are raised too high and they start looking long-term, there's a real inconsistency in them staying together. That was really interesting to play as well."

Losing a couple of scenes in an early episode made the relationship start a little too suddenly for Simcoe. "In 'Picture If You Will', there were scenes in terms of us building up together and we were quite disappointed that we lost them," Simcoe says, "although we lost them for the right reasons. They didn't support the throughline of that episode, but they were real character scenes. They helped develop those two characters into a relationship much more subtly. I think Chiana and D'Argo come together a little bit more

abruptly with the deleting of those scenes."

At the end of 'Die Me, Dichotomy', D'Argo interrupts Chiana and his long-lost son, Jothee, who are about to kiss. Simcoe enjoyed working with Matt Newton, who had previously attended his lectures at the Australian drama school, NIDA. "The relationship with him was great because we got to push some more emotional moments," Simcoe says. "I really believed that he was half-Luxan, which was the main challenge. I didn't want someone to come on board the show who was my son and the only connection be the make-up. I wanted there to be a real psychological and emotional marker that would identify him as being a Luxan, and he got it right. We spent a lot of time talking about the choices that I'd made about Luxans and the changes that I made from the writer's bible. I'd suggest steering it in a particular direction, and Matt did a great job of taking on board Luxan attributes and really owning them for himself."

D'Argo's reason for being on board Moya was to find his son, and Simcoe recognises how dangerous it could be now that he has realised that. "I hope the pay-off works," he says. "It's very difficult giving the super-objective to a long-running character. These things usually pan out over the whole

life of a series, and only get resolved for one or two characters right at the end. I think it was a risky thing to do, and leaves D'Argo in really dangerous territory for season three."

D'Argo's relationships with the other characters are less to the front during the second season. "I think that we accept that the friendship between all the characters has solidified during season two," Simcoe notes. "I think the most telling Crichton/D'Argo scene is in 'Look at the Princess'. There's a scene where Crichton's unsure about going ahead with the wedding, which we jokingly call the 'Obi-Wan Kenobi' scene. Crichton comes to D'Argo for some advice, and the advice he gives is really wise. They have this fantastic chat, and the fact that he came to D'Argo is great. All through that three-parter you get little hooks on how to hang your definition of how that relationship is going. I think in the rest of the season it's a little bit undefined. But they are getting stronger, they are starting to see each other as equals. However, as always with *Farscape*, that's subverted along the way."

Simcoe wishes that there had been more interaction between Aeryn and D'Argo. "Right at the end of season one, when Crichton and everyone is down on the Gammak base, there's a lovely development between them when Aeryn is supposed to be dying on Moya," he points out. "There were some fantastic scenes that could have been pushed through more, but that's the nature of television. You can't explore everything. There's a great sense of respect between them as warriors. I think she didn't rate him at all in season one, but now she sees him as competent. In many ways Crichton, Aeryn, D'Argo and Zhaan all see each other as competent. They may not like the fact that the others are competent, but the real difference between season one and season two is that they have realised that, so they're able to exploit that more."

The layering of the relationships between the characters is one of the joys of working on the series for Simcoe. "I love the fact that the writers haven't pushed D'Argo and Zhaan into a relationship," he says. "If something was just slightly different, then maybe they would have ended up together. They both recognise it, they both feel it, and they both see the lack in themselves exhibited in the other person. There's lots of reasons why they should end up together, but they didn't. I think that's really cool, because when you're chasing storylines for long-running series, a bad way to go is to chase up every street." ■

ZOTOH ZHAAN

Zhaan

"As much as I wish to immerse myself in the Seek and the next level of existence, I cannot abandon you all."

"I think Zhaan is by far the most complicated character on Moya," states Virginia Hey, looking back at the development of the Delvian priest during the second season. "She's always been multi-faceted. The main aim for everybody else in the crew is to go home. Each one has their cultural differences. However, they just have to worry about their own angst and turmoil, getting on with each other to preserve the unity of the crew. Zhaan has all of these things but, in addition, she has this craziness. She has this inner spiritual conflict that can do any number of things: it can fire her up into other facets of her character. She's completely unpredictable."

Hey believes that the conflict within Zhaan remains unresolved. Although she starts to follow the path of the Delvian Seek after she thinks Crichton, Aeryn and D'Argo have died, she reverts to her old ways on their return. "Her spiritual journey didn't cease," Hey hastens to point out. "There's still conflict within her, as there was during the first season. She's constantly battling herself. She's the only Delvian in history who's been able to access her evil side without dying. She wasn't sent crazy and she didn't go through a very ugly, slow death because of the evil. She's been able to actually have this evil surface through her psyche, acknowledge it, and live with it. She knows that's where the conflict lies, I suppose. Human beings on Earth can have an evil side, unfortunately, and live in complete synchronicity with their good side and no one is any the wiser. The Delvians consider experiencing any evil whatsoever to be the worst thing that can ever happen to you. She's in conflict every day. She can have evil thoughts and she can be aggressive. It overwhelms her at times."

Despite this conflict, Zhaan is often a calming presence on board Moya, as Lani Tupu notes: "In a strange way, she's the balance of the team — on a ship of different people, she's the peace keeper." The Delvian develops a new role in the second season as protector of Moya, after she refuses to yield to the Leviathan's Builder, Kahaynu. "Zhaan is a loving, protective, spiritual being who has been given the charge of being responsible for Moya's well-being," Hey says. "That's a weighty task, since Moya and all aboard her are fugitives, forever on the run from the Peacekeepers and constantly in tense situations. Zhaan accepts this charge with the greatest dignity and elegance. She adores Moya and will endeavour to honour it."

Hey also feels that this has given Zhaan a fresh purpose in life. "She was in pain, since she could never go home, having been a political assassin to save her people from the evil dictator," she points out. "If she went

back she would have to murder again, since there's now another evil dictator ruling her planet. She can't bring herself to do that, so here she is rolling aimlessly and painfully in space, albeit supporting her new family's direction. Now she has a personal direction of her own, besides her ongoing spiritual quest. She has to protect Moya at any cost!"

The bond of Unity between Zhaan and Crichton is tested when they encounter Maldis once more. "We share a part of each other," Hey recalls. "In 'Picture If You Will' she went into some kind of Unity with him again." When the Scorpius chip takes over Crichton's brain in 'Die Me, Dichotomy', it takes advantage of that relationship to force Zhaan to release Crichton from his bonds.

By that stage, though, Zhaan has started to forge a relationship with someone else on board — the Stykera Banik Stark. "That's someone who she does love romantically," Hey says. "She loves everybody else. She's a very loving person. She adores Crichton, but it's not sexual, and she flirts with D'Argo, but it's not sexual. With Stark, it's real love. It's a real love affair. We've never seen them do anything more than cuddle. In the scripts they don't ever have us touching but, personally, I'm very affectionate and if I like someone, I'm all over them like a rash! I just brought that part of me into Zhaan's relationship with Stark,

and the directors didn't stop me. In a way, Paul Goddard and I were hoping that the writers would notice that we were getting more and more physical with each other, but I think they wanted to keep their relationship more elegant. Chiana's relationships are very sexual. Zhaan's a very sensual being — sensual rather than sexual."

At the end of 'Die Me, Dichotomy', Stark says that it would be 'an honour and a pleasure to share the future with you.' Hey believes that Stark was proposing marriage to Zhaan. "They're destined to be together forever," she says, "so when he proposed to her I think it was an affirmation of his love. I was very touched, very moved by it."

Although their embrace has featured in the main titles of the first two seasons, Hey doesn't believe that Zhaan and D'Argo have engaged in a sexual relationship. "There's a great affection between us," she explains. "He's a very immature boy, and he and Zhaan have always had a real affection for each other. It was never love. It was always just a warmth for each other. And it's all the way through — it doesn't disappear, it's just that you don't see it every day. But it's not sexual."

Hey believes that even Rygel, deep down, likes the Delvian, despite his regular description of her as a "blue-arsed bitch". "He's not the sort of character that wants to be known as soft at all," she claims. "He's grumpy, bad tempered, ornery and funny, but he adores Zhaan, although he wouldn't ever really show it. He'd much rather insult her, but that doesn't mean he doesn't love her. It's like a wicked brother. He loves you really, but he loves to torture you."

Zhaan has to endure some fairly extreme physical suffering in the second year. "They have a famine so she sickens," Hey explains. "When they're starving, Delvians grow buds which emit spores into the air. The spores affect any flesh and blood creature that's animal, because that's what the Delvians need in time of famine. The spores effectively kill animals that are in the vicinity so they can provide food for the Delvians to eat. I don't know if she would have consumed Crichton and Aeryn, but she was close to it!"

Hey enjoys the character-driven nature of *Farscape*. "That's what makes it so different from other shows," she says. "It's not just driven by special effects, or the visuals, or the storylines. The tension's built in. It's the way the characters interreact. It makes it easier as an actor to have such complicated characters all locked in with each other." ■

CHIANA

Chiana

"Why not just live in the moment? Go fast with the body, slow with the soul."

'Never make assumptions' seems to be the *Farscape* writers' rule, as far as Gigi Edgley can see. "It's very funny to try and assume where your character is going, or where your character is going to end up, because you really have no idea with these guys," she says, clearly loving every minute of the journey. "Just as you think you're getting an idea of your character's emotional journey and how it's all evolving, they'll put this weird twist in it. You can never assume. David Kemper can give you a rough outline of what you're in for, but he'll change it many times. Sometimes it's best not to know at all!"

At the end of the first season, Chiana is still using her physical attributes to try to get her own way, and in the second year we discover that this was how she and her brother Nerri used to operate. "I want there to be a depth to Chiana other than just the physical sultriness of her," Edgley maintains. "In 'Family Ties', the cliffhanger to season one, after she kisses Crichton she says, 'It's the only way I know how to thank you.' You could see that there was a nice, raw essence there. She was falling back on her alien traits. That's how she's grown up — she doesn't know what else to do. It's how she says thank you — and she does tend to say thanks a lot. She's got fantastic manners, you could say!"

As Claudia Black points out, "Crichton is having to deal with a young lady. Chiana could potentially be a lover or a daughter. It really has to plant into his mindset in 'Taking the Stone' that this is a young, unevolved person who isn't an appropriate partner." By this stage, however, there's already a hint that there may be something going on between Chiana and D'Argo.

"We were scraping in little two-line scenes to try and find some sort of chemical reaction," Edgley recalls of those initial faltering indications of attraction. "We wanted the audience to buy the idea that there's an attraction there. It was good to work on the scene in 'Vitas Mortis' where D'Argo's down on the planet, something goes wrong, and she picks up on it. It's nice when they add in those little alien things like telepathy or flying, because it brings you back to the 'reality' of science fiction. When D'Argo walks in with his new Luxan friend and Chiana's trapped in the amnexus fluid, her attitude is, 'You prick, here we are dying on Moya, and you're off rooting and tooting around. I can do that, but you can't!'

"When you put this straight warrior together with this little floozy with a good heart — but everything else has gone goodness knows where — it's a really nice combo to play with," Edgley adds. "I think what I was trying to

create in the relationship was that it was the first time Chiana is actually feeling something a bit deeper. I was trying to find an honesty that comes out, which trips her up the whole time. When you really get close to someone it's the most beautiful thing in life, but it's also the most scary. Sometimes you end up doing really bad things to separate yourself again. So when Chiana goes off and sleazes with someone or fools around — for a very good cause, of course — I would try and justify it by her feeling she was growing too close to D'Argo. She would try to separate herself, because that closeness has never really happened for her before. There's a scene in the neural cluster with D'Argo where she is just caressing him. It's a really beautiful image of this impish thing cuddling this huge warrior creature. He's just immobilised."

Edgley feels that "season two was fantastic for alien characteristics to come out, like the flying and fighting. We found out a bit more about this character who's become part of the crew. It's made her a bit more rock solid." David Kemper enjoys the opportunity to flesh out the characters' backstories, and both 'Home on the Remains' and 'A Clockwork Nebari' revealed new sides of Chiana. "The writers of 'Home on the Remains' and I felt that she

had to exact revenge for what happened to her friends, but we don't want our people committing murder," Kemper says. "It's not right. We don't condone it. We don't foster it, but we had to find a way for her to settle the score, and what we came up with was very satisfying."

"There's a maturity at the end of that episode," Edgley agrees. "I think in that last look she's just blank, and there's so much going through her head. You know she's a thief, you know she's a scoundrel, but you don't know whether she's a red-blooded killer. So when there are those scenes, she loves the adrenaline, but then she thinks, 'Oh my god, what the hell have I done?'

"I see the writers going back into her dark side and diving into this weird pool of emotions inside her," she adds. "She goes on a very intriguing journey to the cliffhanger of season two. I was concerned about some of it, and said to the writers,

'She's been so sweet. She's warmed to the ship quite well, and you want to take her in all these different directions?' and they said, 'Well, it's fantastic to keep pushing you beyond your safety zone!'"

Edgley loves the sense of play on the *Farscape* set, particularly when she and Anthony Simcoe were preparing the 'alien sex' scenes between D'Argo and Chiana. "The very first time you see them playing around, I was a bit nervous," she recalls. "I said to Anthony, 'I'm feeling a bit funny and a little bit bare here. Can we muck around a bit? I want to find out how aliens have sex. I don't want it to be just sex.' So we're mucking around, trying to find some really bizarre way to do it — we were on the floor and upside down, the whole shebang. Andrew Prowse, the director, walks in and says, 'What are you doing?' 'We're having sex!' and he says, 'No, no, stop it, it's got to *look* like you're having sex!' That was supposed to be an even briefer scene than you actually saw. We didn't know how much would be shown. So we ended up doing very simple, what I call 'mundane', movements." Although Simcoe and Edgley had to rein in their impulses on that occasion, Gigi enjoys the sense of freedom that permeates the set: "That's the great thing about *Farscape* — you can literally take things as far as you want, as long as you can justify them for the characters." ■

Rygel

"You all say I'm paranoid, but it's true! No one ever frelling listens to me."

"I think the delight of Rygel is that he does have severe delusions of adequacy," says Jonathan Hardy, who lends his voice to the deposed Hynerian Dominar. "No doubt in Rygel-land, the Hynerian Empire, he was a nasty little despot, but we see him having to come to terms with being ordinary."

Not that Rygel would ever allow anyone to refer to him in such terms. "He doesn't seem as rhetorical as he used to be," Hardy notes. "He seems to have become less imperious and more greedy. I don't know where Ben Browder got the idea of calling him Sparky, but there's obviously been a humanising process going on. There's been a softening, and I regret that he doesn't bite as many people. He certainly doesn't fart helium as much as he used to, although that may be the diet he's on!

"To me, Rygel is good when he can be very active and cunning," Hardy says, "And when he outwits people. That's where his strength lies. He was also very good at diplomacy, although we've gone away from that with him a bit. Naturally," adds the actor with a smile, "I think that when the stories have Rygel in the lead the show peaks, but when Rygel has to support the other actors I think it lacks something!"

Hardy flies in regularly from wherever in the world he is performing to spend hours in the ADR room with engineer Angus Robertson. "I can't tell the difference between me and Rygel any more," Hardy admits. "I go in there, say hello to Angus, and off we go again. I don't try to create Rygel — I just utter him these days."

Hardy jokes that this caused a small problem when he was asked, during the rehearsal period for 'Out of Their Minds', to make his own guide recording of Rygel's lines in the scene where the Hynerian inhabits Crichton's body, for Ben Browder to work from. "I couldn't remember how to do him without Angus there!" Hardy laughs. "I only do Rygel in a small room with Angus."

Part of Hardy's performance is dictated by the physical actions of the puppeteers, and Hardy has noticed a difference since Tim Mieville took over from John Eccleston as chief puppeteer. "Tim is a very different sort of performer from John," he notes. "John was very Mancunian, quite eccentric and difficult to follow. Tim is much more Australian, and he would do things vocally to emphasise lines. That was unnecessary sometimes, and I think he's realised now that he doesn't have to vocally make the drama. I think we've come further and further together."

This was helped by the decision at the start of the second season to improve the lip synchronisation of the puppet. "They wanted to go with a fully animatronic mouth," Tim Mieville explains. "I had been an understudy to Sean Masterson on Pilot, so I had learned how to use the actual hand controls on the rig for the mouth. I stepped up and took over controlling Rygel's mouth.

"The mouth is connected to the brain, so it drives a lot of the text," he adds. "The expressions drive a lot of the subtext and show what Rygel is really thinking. However, they decided that the mouth should be controlling the destiny of the puppet in any scene." Accordingly, Mieville is in charge of Team Rygel and co-ordinates the other puppeteers with the director and the other actors in a scene.

Mieville enjoyed working on the Hannibal Lecter sequence in 'Won't Get Fooled Again' and portraying a mindcleansed Rygel in 'A Clockwork Nebari'. "That was great for us because it meant we could slow everything down," Mieville says, "because he was meant to be stoned, or faking it. Each character had their own version of being mindcleansed, and his was just slowing down. We could relax the eyelids and use a lilting speech pattern. Of course in that same episode he gets found out by Crichton, and has various moments of his usual panic and scaredy-catness."

Mat McCoy, who has his hand physically inside the Rygel puppet, thinks that Team Rygel is evolving with the demands that are being placed upon them by the writers. "I think we got so good, it encouraged the writers to think, 'why don't we put him in this situation?'" he says. "That's great, because I like that development of the character. Rygel has been a prisoner on the ship the longest. All this horrible stuff has happened to him, and he still isn't dead. The whole ship could explode and Rygel would find a way of getting off it alive! It's good when they explore those sides of him. The pettiness and the greed are there, and there's the hardness that he needs to survive, but also a softness too. I like the idea that, as his character has developed, you start to see him as the leader he could have been. I love to think of what it would be like if Rygel went back to Hyneria — it would be weird."

Tim Mieville also appreciates the development of Rygel's self-reliance. "We've seen

Above: Jonathan Hardy records Rygel's lines.

Durka in three episodes," he says, recalling the Hynerian's former torturer. "The first was in a flashback in 'PK Tech Girl', when he still freaked Rygel out. In 'Durka Returns', Rygel confronted him, and you can see Rygel decide that Durka is as much a bluffer as he is. He knows what this guy is about, and he thinks he can sort him out, which he does, to a certain extent. The third time, in 'Liars, Guns and Money', when he's with the Zenetans, Durka is all bluff with Rygel, but Rygel has decided what he's going to do — he lets him get in close, then he gives him a zap and kills him!"

All the puppeteers believe that the more the actors interact with the puppets, the more the puppets become real. This does sometimes lead to Rygel being physically abused. "It affects people when they see something that looks no bigger than a four year-old child getting smashed around so much," Mieville admits, "but we figure he's more like a chimpanzee. Chimps can fall from a height of thirty feet, land on their stomach and walk away without a problem. Their tolerance for pain is a lot higher. Rygel's physiognomy is a lot stronger than you'd think. He's not used to doing the work, of course, because he is the Dominar, but he can use his strength when he needs to. I think we can justify that he doesn't most of the time by the simple fact that he is a lazy son of a bitch!" ■

"The Builders placed our fates in your care, Zhaan. Whatever you decide, we will abide by it."

lthough during the first season Pilot claimed that he and Moya were happiest when serving, it becomes clear during *Farscape*'s second year that this is not the whole story. Moya can place personal considerations ahead of others, and it emerges that Pilot was ruthless enough to allow another of his race to be murdered in order to fulfil his dreams.

After Talyn's birth in 'The Hidden Memory', Moya discovers that her priorities have changed. Although she was prepared to risk StarBurst in 'Through the Looking Glass' rather than lose the crew, in season two's 'Dream a Little Dream' she insists on calling off the search for the missing Crichton, Aeryn and D'Argo, and starts to look for Talyn. "Moya's in full lunatic-mother mode," Chiana says in 'Mind the Baby', when Moya persists in her search "despite the risk" that Pilot notes.

The birth of her gun-ship offspring almost costs Moya her life when she encounters her god, Kahaynu the Builder. "We created these beasts as emissaries of peace," Kahaynu tells Zhaan and, although he agrees the Leviathan is a gentle soul, she nevertheless "is able to reproduce ships that can dispense carnage", which is forbidden by the Builders. Though Moya was not to blame for Talyn's weapons, she feels responsible, so, not wanting to disobey her creator, the Leviathan starts to shut down her own systems. When Kahaynu grants Moya voice, she tells Zhaan "Moya go... willing." However, Kahaynu was actually testing Zhaan's worthiness: "These are gentle beasts who will ultimately follow the directions of those in control. Should you desire it, priestess, you could produce an army of killing machines." Pilot protests that Zhaan would never do such a thing and Kahaynu agrees. "We know that now. We are confident that you will protect Moya vigorously against those who seek to exploit her." Later, Moya implicitly trusts Zhaan when the Delvian tells her, in order to get rid of the Karack metallites, she needs to be burned, since she believes that Kahaynu handed over responsibility for her fate to the Delvian.

Moya maintains a mother's interest in Talyn, asking, through Pilot, about his growth in 'Out of Their Minds'. When they meet again in 'The Ugly Truth', Pilot reports that Moya is "pleased that he's healthy and happy". When Talyn StarBursts away after destroying the Plokavian ship, Moya anxiously tries to find him, and eventually Pilot reports that she is doing so from a sense of guilt. "She feels responsible for what he does," he tells Chiana. It is only when Chiana appeals to Moya's sense of responsibility for the crew, especially Zhaan and Aeryn, that she agrees to return for them. It transpires that Talyn was trying to protect Moya from the

Novatrin gas that the Plokavian arms dealers were carrying.

Moya has a lifespan of around 300 cycles as opposed to Pilot's 1,000, but Pilot accepts that he will die if he is disconnected from Moya, either willingly or through her death. However, although she and Pilot share a symbiotic closeness, the current Pilot was not her first. Refusing to take part in Crais's genetic experiments, Pilot's predecessor was killed by a Peacekeeper team that included Aeryn Sun and the current Pilot was put in place. The Command Collar that Moya wore while in the service of the Peacekeepers was used to give the Leviathan a pain pulse that forced her to accept the replacement. When the truth is revealed, Pilot disconnects himself in guilt, but a natural bonding follows, allowing Pilot and the Leviathan to achieve their full potential.

In 'The Way We Weren't', we learn that Pilot was judged by the Elders of his species, who told him he was not yet worthy to pilot a Leviathan. He therefore came to a private deal with Peacekeeper Velorek, who offered him the chance to see the galaxy in exchange for his co-operation. "If I hadn't agreed to come, Velorek may never have found a replacement Pilot," the symbiont tells Aeryn. "But I just wanted so desperately to see the stars."

Lani Tupu, who voices Pilot, points out that "up until then, Pilot is the pure navigator. His attitude was one of total service. But we discover in that episode that he's not as innocent as you want him to be, or as he pretends to be. He made a choice to have the stars."

"Initially everyone always says he's the pacifist," says Sean Masterson, who is in charge of the team operating Pilot. "'The Way We Weren't' was a great way of seeing him in depth. All of a sudden, Pilot wasn't quite understandable any more. The character was unveiled. It was like peeling an onion and finding something completely different underneath."

Pilot is able to communicate in both very simple and very complex ways. He can understand the Vorc because his bond with Moya makes him accustomed to non-verbal communication. However, in the ancient language of his own species, one sentence can carry over a hundred different facts, concepts, or emotions. In order to speak to others, he has to simplify his sentences.

That makes life easier for Masterson and his team. It takes anything up to seven people to work Pilot, depending on what the scene calls on him to do. "I do the lip sync in the characterisation, so

I'll say the lines on set and use a hand-operated device called a Waldo, which makes lip sync patterns," Masterson explains. "Beside me is Mat McCoy, who does all the eye expressions. Inside the puppet is Mario Halouvas, who has a couple of bars and controls the gross movement of the head: the large swings, the nods and the shakes. He's also harnessed into it so he can move the body. Tim Mieville and Fiona Gentile work the arms with others when we need them. We all have to work together as a strict unit," he adds. "We have to break each scene down so that each person adds bits and pieces until the whole picture is there. We've worked together as a team now for so long that we're all pretty well clued into what each person is thinking."

Masterson loves working with Pilot. "He's the Maserati of puppets," he says, "and he's a great character. I like the innocence about him, and yet underneath it all is this real hardness, which only comes out in the really dark episodes. This wonderful character, who everyone loves, is basically a little treacherous. The whole team had a great time with 'The Way We Weren't'. All the other characters get on very well with the puppet characters, and there's an especially good relationship between Aeryn and Pilot. To suddenly undo a year and a half of character development between the two of them was great fun."

For Lani Tupu, the growth of Pilot and the other members of Moya's crew as characters is simply "a gift from the writers. It's all in the writing," he explains. "They give us the notes and we play the music. It's all there. And because we have such a history with these characters, we don't really have to push it. We just let it play. The wonderful thing now is that we can bring in elements of subtlety, because the audience knows the characters' history." ■

Opposite page: Sean Masterson (left) and Mat McCoy operate Pilot.

Tony Tilse

"It was wild to look round the room and see all these characters we'd brought back."

Rather than engaging in an all-encompassing pursuit of John Crichton, similar to Crais's obsession during the first season, Scorpius is often a background presence, stalking the Earth astronaut. He is as determined as ever to obtain the wormhole technology from the human's subconscious, but the reason for his patience is only revealed halfway through the season. While Crichton was in the Aurora Chair in season one's 'The Hidden Memory', Scorpius implanted a clone chip of himself into Crichton's brain, with a directive to protect Crichton from danger while it searches the human's brain for the wormhole information. Once this has been located, the clone is programmed to take control of Crichton's body and bring the information to the half-breed.

Scorpius is so sure of his eventual victory that he is more than happy to stop along the way to engage in the odd bit of torture, profiteering, or even an amorous encounter with his lover, the crustaceous Shadow Depository owner, Natira. With Crais out of the way, Scorpius has taken over the Peacekeeper Captain's Command Carrier and has forged a close unit of loyal Peacekeeper soldiers, who both fear him and are revolted by his half-breed nature. However, he can show a surprising level of forgiveness to those that fail him.

Scorpius

"I condemn you, John Crichton, to live. So that your thirst for unfulfilled revenge will consume you. Goodbye."

The hybrid himself has a weakness: the cooling rods implanted within his head. Scorpius's mixed Scarran-Sebacean physiology means that his body temperature must be strictly controlled. The rods need regular changing by a nurse Scorpius keeps in attendance, although extra pressures, particularly sensual, can speed up the rate at which they are depleted. It transpires that Tocot — the Diagnosan who attempts to remove the clone from Crichton's brain in 'Die Me, Dichotomy' — was earlier responsible for the creation of Scorpius's bizarre cooling system.

During *Farscape*'s second year, we see more of Scorpius's clone persona than of the scientist himself. However, the congeniality that the clone displays — wearing multi-coloured shirts, discussing Margarita shooters or playing chess with Crichton — makes the original all the more frightening when he makes his irregular appearances.

Farscape's second season brought new opportunities for Wayne Pygram, who plays both Scorpius and his clone. "I don't want to soften Scorpius, but the clone is a chance to laugh at him," he points out. "He has a different energy."

The actor was unaware of how important the clone would become when

the persona made his first appearance in 'Crackers Don't Matter'. "It started in a very naïve way — how does Scorpius get the information? He puts a clone in," he explains. "They thought that they might as well have the clone be physical in Crichton's subconscious, but I don't think that was the original idea. It was evolving all the time."

Pygram is grateful on a practical level for the clone's creation. "If you see too much of Scorpius, he loses his venom," he explains. "I think the Scorpius clone is a great idea for driving drama and creating interest. Some of the Scorpy clone stuff is pure embellishment, added in after the main thread of the episode has been developed. To me it feels like, 'What can they do with Wayne?' So they give me a scene or two in Crichton's subconscious to keep me in it. The clone wasn't a fully realised idea at first, but it was developed as the year went on."

The 'Liars, Guns and Money' trilogy showed other sides to Scorpius, which Pygram particularly enjoyed. "I see Scorpius as a bastard child," he says. "He was not wanted. At birth no one would have wanted him to live, but somehow he survived. He doesn't have any friends, or a sense of loyalty. He is always suspicious, he's always on his guard. Everyone is someone who could smother him."

By the end of the second year, **Stark** has become a full-time member of Moya's crew, but only a little more is learned about the Banik former slave. He does reveal that he is a Stykera, someone who is attuned to the dying, and can sense when large numbers of his race are killed simultaneously. He also explains that his body is merely a link into this reality, and that his true existence is in another realm, in the form of energy. Stark first suggests this in 'The Ugly Truth', just prior to his dispersal by the Plokavians, in an attempt to comfort and reassure the rest of the crew, but no one believes him. It is hardly surprising then that, when Zhaan declares that Stark has returned, she is met with scepticism. He is greeted with a mixture of joy and mistrust, but the details of his plan to rescue D'Argo's son override the crew's interest in how he managed to survive dispersal.

> **Stark**
>
> "If you are in agreement, Pa'u Zotoh Zhaan, it would be an honour and a pleasure to share the future with you."

With the Banik back on board Moya, John Crichton isn't the only one whose sanity seems somewhat unstable, but Stark's inconsistent and erratic behaviour is harder to explain, as he alternates between lying to the crew, throwing tantrums and 'faking' his madness. One thing that does become clear, however, is that Stark and Zhaan share more than spiritual beliefs. After they join in Unity to save the crew in 'The Locket', a deep bond of affection quickly develops between them, culminating in Stark's proposal to stay with the Delvian at the end of the season.

Paul Goddard, who originally auditioned for the role of Scorpius, made his first appearance as Stark in season one's 'Nerve'. His initial take on the

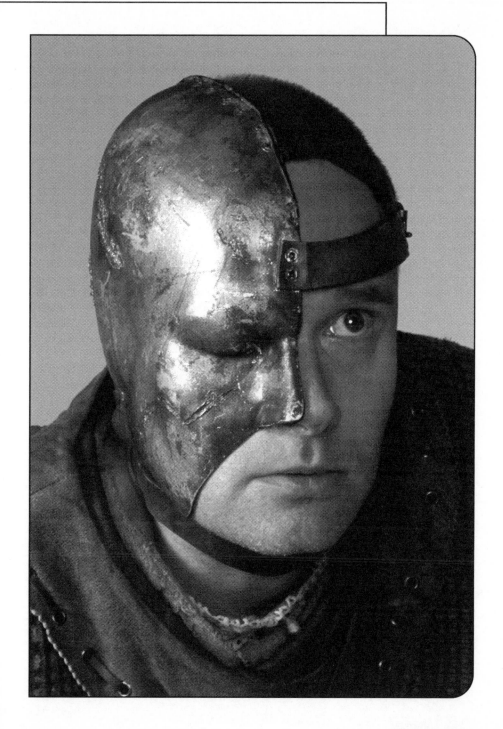

character was based on performances he had seen in *One Flew Over the Cuckoo's Nest*, and Brad Pitt's unhinged character in *Twelve Monkeys*. "I feel Stark's sanity is in a state of flux all the time," Goddard explains. "Partly because sanity can be like that, and partly because if you're an alien, what would your normal behaviour be anyway? If we had a whole load of Baniks on board, you might find that they're equally as scatty, nervous and highly-strung as he is. Initially, the madness that he had was thought to be a pretence in order to protect himself, like a defence mechanism.

"When I came back, in 'The Locket', Stark seemed quite sane, but the producers and I talked about how good it would be not to lose all of the madness. He can use it either as a defence mechanism or, in situations of high stress, he'll be fine and then he'll just slip. We also mentioned the possibility that he may use it as a ruse with the crew as well, not just with his enemies. The question is, just how much is put on, and how much is genuine? It's like somebody who's ill, and bemoans their lot. You wonder how much is attention seeking and how much is a genuine expression of their pain.

"The burgeoning romance with Zhaan, I think, has grounded him a bit," Goddard adds. "When he's with Zhaan he shows his more relaxed, spiritual side. I thought it would be a little ridiculous if I was this scatty child-like creature all the time when I'm with her, and that guided me in the relationship."

When Peacekeeper captain **Bialar Crais** steals Moya's baby Talyn in 'Family Ties', the crew believes that they have seen the last of him. But Crais soon returns, to play a dangerous game of double and triple bluff with Aeryn and Scorpius, helping Aeryn rescue Crichton and D'Argo from certain death while pretending to be assisting Scorpius in finding Crichton. When Talyn chooses to offer the Hand of Friendship to Crais rather than Aeryn at the end of 'Mind the Baby', he disappears into the Uncharted Territories with the Peacekeeper-Leviathan hybrid ship. Since Crais was responsible for the Peacekeeper experiment on Moya that led to Talyn's birth, he wants to possess and master his creation.

> **Crais**
>
> "My parents were compassionate, moral, emotional. I value those traits."

During the year, the crew of Moya encounter Crais and Talyn on several occasions. Each time, Crais proclaims that he has Talyn's best interests at heart, and will assist the crew to the greater good of the two Leviathans. Whether his actions are those of nurturing or enslavement is something that is never clear; his motivations in 'The Ugly Truth' remain unexplained at the end of the episode. However, Crais is the only person Talyn completely trusts, even over Aeryn.

In the first season, Crais's hunt for Crichton is what keeps the crew on the run. "I don't think at the beginning of season two John is positively disposed to Crais," Ben Browder notes. "But by the end of the season, Crais as a threat, or

having any kind of relationship to John, is superseded by the fact that John is going insane. John's got Scorpius in his head — who cares about Crais?"

Lani Tupu sees the relationship between Crais and Crichton developing into a form of respect from the former Peacekeeper: "I think the relationship will always be tense, and I guess that's the way it should be. We're really shooting this epic, filmic story. It feels as if we've gone a step up from normal television production. The characters drive the story. There are wonderful nuances in the characters, as they learn to live with each other under extraordinary circumstances.

"I really love the scene in 'Die Me, Dichotomy' when Crichton is on the slab," Tupu adds, "and Crais sees how brave he really is. There is a definite respect there, and there's a reaction shot where you can see all the stuff that's happening in Crais's head."

As for Talyn, Tupu believes that, at first, Crais saw the young warship as a pupil: "Crais has an opportunity to teach Talyn the arts of strategy and warfare. Then Talyn shows Crais a few things as well! It's a sort of symbiotic relationship, and Crais starts off in a teaching capacity, but as Talyn grows, they become more like parent and child.

"Children are always a mixture of both parents. They have the qualities of both, and somewhere along the line, they begin to experience the world, develop their own qualities, and become these amazing beings. That's really what Talyn is. He eventually makes decisions of his own, even though Crais is there."

Despite D'Argo's repeated visions of a bitter and unforgiving son, when they are finally reunited, **Jothee** declares his never-wavering faith that his father would find and rescue him. Jothee also reassures D'Argo that he never blamed him for his banishment to a life of slavery. However, all is not well with Jothee. He carries both mental and physical scars, some of which are self-inflicted. He swings between loving the father he knew would save him, and simultaneously hating him for orchestrating the situation that resulted in the death of a woman they both loved, and years of internment and misery for them both. Although Jothee rejoices at his reunion with his father, he quickly discovers that their paths do not lie together, as his dreams of adventure couldn't be further from his father's plans for a tranquil existence.

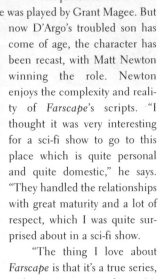

Jothee

"I have done things, many things I am not proud of, to survive. I only just got my freedom back. I'm not going to risk losing it again."

In the first season, the young Jothee was played by Grant Magee. But now D'Argo's troubled son has come of age, the character has been recast, with Matt Newton winning the role. Newton enjoys the complexity and reality of *Farscape*'s scripts. "I thought it was very interesting for a sci-fi show to go to this place which is quite personal and quite domestic," he says. "They handled the relationships with great maturity and a lot of respect, which I was quite surprised about in a sci-fi show.

"The thing I love about *Farscape* is that it's a true series, with continuing storylines. It's like a soap opera in a way. Each episode finishes on a high note, and you don't know what's going to happen. In the next episode one question gets answered, but another one gets asked. I really like the way that things aren't resolved cleanly. They are resolved like they are in real life."

When the real Scorpius is on the scene, so is his loyal Lieutenant, **Braca**. The Sebacean is the classic henchman, but with one vital difference — Scorpius does not have him eliminated whenever he fails, which is on a regular basis where Crichton is concerned. Braca has managed to corner the Earthman on a number of occasions, but hasn't succeeded in capturing him. When faced with Crichton on a one-to-one basis, as in 'Look at the Princess', he becomes confused and hesitant. Whether this is due to Crichton's induced madness or Braca's lack of experience with alien creatures is something that has yet to be revealed.

> **Braca**
>
> " Sit down, or I'll shoot your limbs off one at a time."

"I think he's survived by the skin of his teeth!" says Australian actor David Franklin, who has played Braca since season one's 'The Hidden Memory'. "He gets into a situation with Scorpius and he thinks, 'How do I survive this? What's the right thing to say? Do I take this attitude?' He's always covering his back."

Chris Haywood returns as the malevolent magician **Maldis** to threaten the crew in 'Picture If You Will'. Trying to re-enter the real world from the realm to which he had been sent at the end of season one's 'That Old Black Magic', Maldis lays an elaborate trap. He manipulates matter to create an interstellar trader, Kyvan, who sells a mysterious painting to Chiana. The painting is a bridge between the realms, and also creates an atmosphere of fear from which the psychic vampire can feed. He then plans to capture the crew one by one and transport them to his realm, where he can exact his revenge on Zhaan for defeating him. But the Delvian suspects that Maldis is behind the scheme, and feigns weakness in order to dupe him into underestimating her. Maldis ends up trapped once more.

Maldis

"Have you forgotten?
Fear makes me stronger.
Fear and the terror
of helplessness.
These are a few of my
favourite things."

The return of **Selto Durka** (played by David Wheeler) is brief but memorable. When Rygel approaches the Zenetan pirates from 'The Flax' in order to gain their help in the raid on the Shadow Depository in 'Liars, Guns and Money', he is surprised to find that Durka is now their leader. However, after standing up to him in 'Durka Returns', Rygel no longer fears his former torturer, and kills him, cutting off the Sebacean's head and carrying it with him on a pole as a keepsake! The other Zenetan pirates, led by Zelkin, then join forces with Moya's crew, although they eventually try to betray them to Scorpius.

Also required for the raid is **Bekhesh**, the Tavlek warrior seen in the first season's 'Throne for a Loss'. However, when Crichton finds the warrior, portrayed by John Adam, he has given up his ways of violence for a life of religious contemplation, and it takes the human some considerable time to persuade the Tavlek to put on his gauntlet and return to the fray.

D'Argo's assignment is to find the Vorcarian Blood Trackers **Rorf** and **Rorg**, once again played by Jeremy Sims and Jo Kerrigan, from 'Till the Blood Runs Clear'. Rorg is pregnant and so it is left to her mate to assist with the raid. When Rorf is captured he is tortured by Natira and loses one of his eyes, before giving his life in the final battle to rescue Crichton.

> **Crichton**
>
> " Alright, here's the deal. We have minimal weapons, no way to hide from Scorpius. If we're going to surprise him, we've got to get some help."

Aeryn, meanwhile, finds **Teurac**, one of the Sheyang responsible for attacking Moya when they encountered the Zelbinion in 'PK Tech Girl'. Now played by Thomas Holesgrove (and voiced by Phillip Hinton), Teurac has been abandoned by his crew, and Aeryn fears that he is weak and used up. Proud to be associated with the raid, Teurac tries to hide his impotence at fire breathing, and finally takes Taakar serum in order to feed his flame — knowing that this will probably lead to his death, as it ultimately does.

THE EFFECTS

FULL SCARRON WITH MASK
DAVE ELSEY
CREATURE SHOP

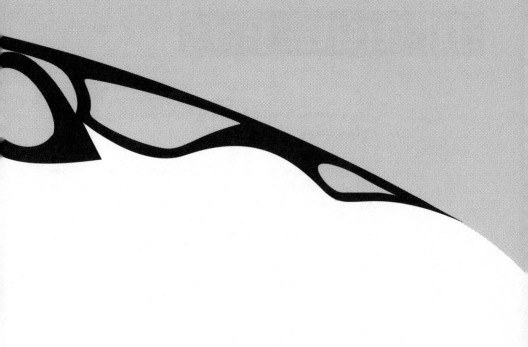

"Can someone please tell me what the yotz I'm looking at?"

– Rygel

Sue Milliken

"The Creature Shop is inventing the wheel every episode, with something completely new."

When he knew that *Farscape* was returning for a second year, creative supervisor Dave Elsey and his crew at the Sydney Creature Shop reviewed the various make-ups for the main characters. Luckily, the first episode to be filmed, 'Dream a Little Dream', didn't need too much new work from his team. "It was a very slow start to the beginning of the year," Elsey recalls. "The Litigarans were really only small make-up jobs. So we decided to review Scorpius and D'Argo from scratch, and we started work on a new Rygel puppet, updating the skins and everything. We started off very simple and we ended up over-complicating everything!"

D'Argo was the first to undergo changes, with a new, slightly darker skin tone. "We wanted to colour him better for the camera," Elsey explains. Always on the look-out for an explanation in the script or a character's backstory for its appearance, Elsey reckoned that since D'Argo had last been seen floating in space at the end of 'Family Ties', he had devel-

oped a "Luxan space tan. Maybe the pressure of being in space had forced the blood to the surface."

Elsey is much happier with the Luxan's look for the second year. "I resculpted D'Argo during the first two weeks of the season because I wanted to get everything a bit finer, and get a little more movement out of it. We did lots of streamlining."

The Rygel puppet underwent a more fundamental change. With a change in puppeteer from John Eccleston to Team Rygel, Elsey decided to alter the whole way the puppet was used. "We updated his mechanisms and got his expressions working a lot more smoothly," he says. "On the first season, Rygel was basically a hand puppet. The puppeteer had his hand in Rygel's head, and his jaw was the guy's thumb. Whenever I looked at it, all I could see was the thumb moving around under the skin, which irritated me.

"We updated the fully remote version, which we had built, but not used, on season one. Rygel is now a mixture of hand puppet and fully remote, so you don't need to have millions of cables coming to a big cable control. The guy who's moving the head is now not moving the lips. He can concentrate on making the head look in the right direction. Somebody else is looking at a monitor off camera, and using the Henson Control System to operate the facial expression. Everybody is in charge of their own bit."

Opposite page: Zoe Skinner prepares Rygel for action.

Above: Tim Mieville at the Henson Control System.

The new puppet received a baptism of fire in 'Crackers Don't Matter'. "Of course Anthony Simcoe nearly destroyed the Rygel puppet by forcing crackers into his mouth, despite me telling him again and again to be careful with it," Elsey says ruefully. "Even in rehearsals he couldn't wait to smash as many of the real crackers into Rygel's mouth as possible. It was like a *Sesame Street* gag. Crumbs were going everywhere. I don't mind, because all of our puppets have to go through that. You can almost guarantee that as soon as we change the skin on a puppet, the first thing they'll do is dunk it in water, or sling it in mud. It's one of those things that just has to happen." Far from annoying Elsey, he actually loves scenes like this. "I like to see Rygel get abused, because I think it's one of the best things about *Farscape*. It just cracks me up when the puppet gets smashed up!"

The most noticeable changes were to Scorpius. Because the Scarran-Sebacean half-breed had only been in four season one episodes, Elsey felt able to go back and make some major alterations to Wayne Pygram's makeup. "We resculpted the whole thing," Elsey says. "We improved some of the

moulds because we came up with some different ideas. The Hot Flesh process [the special translucent compound used for the make-up] was still in its infancy, and we'd come up with some different ideas, so we wanted to try out some new moulds. We also wanted to make the helmet secure onto Wayne's head slightly differently, and we changed the way he was actually put into the make-up. There's now a little black hood that goes on under his leather hood and under his 'face'. Somebody kept saying that Scorpius's face was like fish skin, or your finger after you've taken a plaster off, and that just stuck with me, so we gave his face more of a sheen and pushed that idea a little bit further. I also felt his helmet didn't match. The rest of his costume had a very high gloss on it, and I wanted to tie those things together. So we basically tightened the make-up and made it fit Wayne better."

Scorpius's appearance in 'Mind the Baby' also marked the first time that we saw the cooling rod coming out of his head. Elsey is very proud that this idea came from the Creature Shop. The episode's director, Andrew Prowse, wanted Scorpius's new nurse to "do some sort of business on his head, and it didn't really matter what it was," Elsey remembers. "Wayne came to us and asked what we could do. My colleague Colin Ware and I decided that, even though there was only a week left until it had to be in front of the cameras, we would try to make the most of it, and we came up with the whole concept. It would be an egg whisk-type thing containing cooling rods, which shoots right out of Scorpius's head — it was obviously implanted right in his brain, and it was clearly a very painful procedure. Andrew Prowse was a bit concerned that it was so big and came out quite so far from Wayne's head. He wasn't convinced about the twisting out idea either. We said that it should look horrible, like it's mincing up his brain as it comes out. Nobody was too enamoured with it at first, but the rest is history: everybody loves it now and it became a major part of the Scorpy tale. I'm pretty sure there was no mention of it in the script at the time. It's just one of those lucky things that happens on *Farscape*, where everything turns out right on the day. We're quite pleased that it all came from our discussion in a cab on the way home!"

One of the most striking creatures from the early part of the season was Traltixx, the blind alien mechanic from 'Crackers Don't Matter'. "David Kemper asked me very early on to design a character who was blind, and had no eyes at all," Elsey says. "I thought it sounded interesting. I had wanted to include a tribute to 1950s-style aliens, so that was how we approached it. They wanted something that was so wrinkled you couldn't see the eyes. Then the wrinkles would part and you would eventually see the creature's eyes underneath, glowing. That sounded a bit boring: I wanted to design something more challenging. I wanted something that looked as if it once had eyes, and then they had simply healed over. However, we also knew we had to have the glowing eyes appear at some point, so we used translucent skin. The light would come through in different places, so the eyes wouldn't necessarily be where you'd think they would be."

Placing the eyes caused a technical problem for Elsey's crew: "A lot of times when you have eyes where they shouldn't be on a make-up or an animatronic head — and Traltixx was half animatronic, half make-up — you end up having to put little holes in the face, so the actors can actually see through them. We didn't want to do this: I couldn't bring myself to put little black holes in freckles all over the face, so the actor could look out. We checked into the possibility of using virtual reality goggles, but they were too expensive.

"So we racked our brains for ages trying to think of a clever idea. We knew we were going to be breaking the head into two — the top half was going to lift off and the bottom half would be glued on permanently. Then I remembered those cardboard periscopes you could buy when I was a kid. Two mirrors had got to be cheaper than VR goggles! So we got a couple of mirrors, played about with them, and it worked really well. Because Traltixx has a 'breathing unit' where we were dividing the make-up from the animatronic, we incorporated the periscope into the top of his head. So the actor is actually looking out of the top of his head, into a little grid through that mechanical unit at the top that the character is 'breathing' through. The effect onscreen was really good, and we're quite proud of that."

Opposite page:
Scorpius's make-up was revised for season two.

Above: Testing Traltixx's glowing eyes.

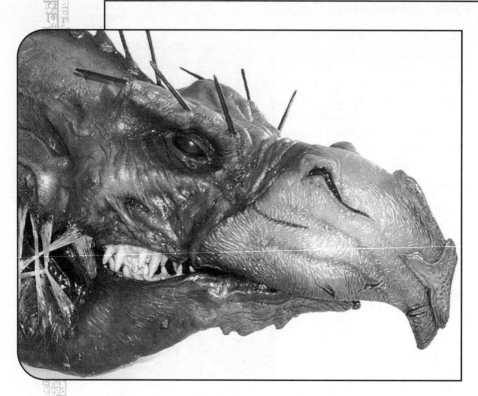

Vision, or lack of it, is often a problem for those wearing the Creature Shop's creations. Thomas Holesgrove, who played no less than five different roles during the second year, started on the show as Yoz, one of the bird-like Halosians in 'Out of Their Minds'. "That was the hardest creature to work," Holesgrove says. "It was very difficult. It had a backpack with a metal spine, with the head on the end of that. You're puppeteering the head, which is very tricky because you can never see anything. The creature's eyes are nowhere near your own eyes. It was quite a strain to have that metal bar on your shoulders and your arms. To get into the costume there was a hole, and once you were zipped up inside, your arms were stuck."

With benefit of hindsight, Elsey admits that he probably wouldn't attempt anything as complicated as the Halosians again on a television schedule. "We were asked to design very bird-like characters. We thought this would be a great time to pay homage to Jim Henson and *The Dark Crystal*, so we designed creatures like the Skeksis," he says, referring to the creatures in the 1983 movie. "They're actually not very similar — if you put them together, they're a completely different size. I hope the Halosians never come back! The worst thing about them was that I was very pleased with them in the workshop. You can do something in the workshop that looks great and works fantastically well. However, the moment it's on set and you have people puppeteering things, and they're pointing a camera at it, and trying to get it into impossible positions that it can't function properly in, it suddenly doesn't look as good."

Another problem that faced the Creature Shop constantly in the second year was the incredible heat on the Homebush Bay sound stages during the Australian summer. Thinking back to the Keedva in 'Home on the Remains', Elsey says, "It helped that it was furry, which hid the things that we had to hide, but it's true that I designed the furriest creature we'd used on *Farscape* for the worst week of summer!"

The bifurcated-headed B'Sogg from that episode was one of the more unusual humanoid characters of the year. Elsey recalls that director Rowan Woods wanted something a little off-key. "They wanted all the characters to be terribly scarred, as if they'd all been involved in terrible mining accidents," he says. "They wanted B'Sogg to be the most alien and the most scarred of all. So we came up with that head cleft that he has, and Rowan was delighted when he saw it.

"We also had to kill B'Sogg and have his arm melt off. For that we used Hot Flesh. We had discovered that you can melt Hot Flesh with chemicals that are not harmful to the human body. We created a glove that was very skinny, with elongated fingers, made of foam latex impregnated with silicate as an extra precaution. That was then made to look like bone and muscle. Over the top of that we sculpted a melted version of B'Sogg's hand, made of Hot Flesh. Into that we pumped chemicals that ate away the Hot Flesh but didn't eat away at the glove underneath, so you could get a really good hand movement as the thing started to pump. And we dyed it red too, so it would be like blood.

"You could see the whole thing disintegrate. You'd never seen anything moving quite the way it did. We did about three or four takes, and we were very pleased with that. It was the most horrific thing that we've made for *Farscape*. The last time I did anything as gory as that was when I worked on

Opposite page: Close-up of a Halosian.

Above: The Keedva is readied for filming by Zoe Skinner (left) and Lou Elsey.

Next page: The bifurcated B'Sogg.

Page 137: The Scarran featured in 'Won't Get Fooled Again'.

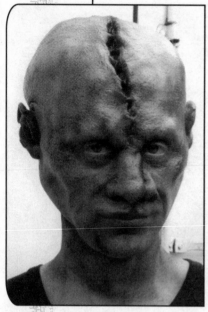

Hellraiser [Clive Barker's celebrated 1987 horror film]. We also did a scene where B'Sogg's hand was cut off and the blood was all over the wall, but it was all out of focus in the episode. We just see him waving his stump around in the background."

One of the major species that made their début during the second year was the Scarran. A Scarran diplomat appeared in the three-part 'Look at the Princess', although he wasn't quite as Dave Elsey originally envisioned the race. "We knew we were going to be creating Scarrans further along the line, because it was quite obvious from Scorpius's backstory that they were going to be quite important," he says. "We designed the Scarran diplomat to be a little more portly, a bit slower than the Scarrans we saw later on in the season. Even though he's still a vicious creature, he's quite a different type from what we see later on with the proper Scarrans."

The Scarran suit proved to be a problem during the filming of 'Look at the Princess', not helped by the fierce heat on location in Sydney's Chinese Gardens. As director Andrew Prowse recalls, one of the actors only discovered when he was in the suit that he was claustrophobic. Dave Elsey points out that this was one of the difficulties with filming a show like *Farscape* in Australia. "In England or the States, you have a stock company of performers who you know are able to go into costume and suits, and do very difficult work under very tough conditions," he explains. "They're known as suit performers. Out here, that doesn't really exist yet. It's just starting now, and we've had to find people to go into all of our suits from scratch. Because there's not really time to do a lot of research, you can only test the performers out onscreen. We went through three or four different people on 'Look at the Princess' — there were loads of reasons why they didn't work. However, we have been lucky, because we've found Thomas Holesgrove, who is excellent in suits, and has become our main 'creature guy' now. We've made casts of every single part of his body."

A Scarran reappeared as the villain of the piece in the surreal episode 'Won't Get Fooled Again', played by Holesgrove. "We knew that this was where we were going to see the Scarran properly," Elsey says. "It was much more like my original painting of the Scarran with all the bondage gear."

Creating that Scarran led to a change in the way costumes and creatures were designed for the show. Previously, the costume department had been responsible for clothing the creatures, and the Creature Shop would deal with

the hands, head or body that were required. Often, this would mean creating a 'muscle suit' which changed the physique of the person wearing it, and the costume would then have to fit over that new shape. This caused some delays on set, since the costume department had to remove their outfit before the Creature Shop could remove theirs.

"We decided to try and simplify the process," Dave Elsey says. "My wife, Lou, is a costume designer, and does all the muscle suits, which are very complicated. We wanted to show muscles moving about under the skin with the Scarrans, but we also wanted the costume to be as tight-fitting as we could make it. But we still had to get Thomas in and out in fifteen minutes, which is the time allotted to us to get people in and out of costumes. So Lou took my designs, and did the costume designs on the Scarran as well as the muscle suit. It meant that we were able to get him in and out of costume very quickly, and because we had control over the whole thing, it homogenised the look of the creature. I was very pleased with the way that turned out, and it's the way that we've done some things ever since. If we do a make-up, or something where we're just changing the actor's head and hands, then Terry Ryan does what he normally does with the costumes. However, if we start to change the bodyshape, which means we're getting into much more complicated areas, then we do the costumes as well."

A particularly memorable effect seen during the second year was the removal of John Crichton's eyes during the Nebari mind-cleansing process in 'A Clockwork Nebari'. Writer Lily Taylor told Dave Elsey that she wanted to do something similar to the scene in the movie *A Clockwork Orange*, where Malcolm McDowell's character Alex has his eyes held open as he's forced to watch films on a screen.

Elsey knew immediately that they wouldn't be able to hold Ben Browder's eyes open forcibly, as McDowell's had been in Stanley Kubrick's movie. It occurred to him to take advantage of the compositing process, where different visual effects are put together on the computer. "I started to think it would be nice if we could remove Crichton's eyeballs altogether from his head," he says. "I wanted to find a way to do that which would be different from what you might have seen before. I didn't want to do a fake head, because if it's not done brilliantly, it would look pretty dreadful. So I decided to make a head with a false section on it, based on Ben's face, and he wore goggles which masked the join. We shot his eyes on another stage, separate from the rest of his face, with the whole Nebari torture device shot separately as well, and then combined it all together in post-production. It took a lot of working out and many discussions. People were worried it might be too much, but as always with anything that involves an idea taken to excess on *Farscape*, we did it. It turned out really cool!"

A real highlight of the season was the appearance of Natira, Scorpius's lover, in the 'Liars, Guns and Money' trilogy. But the creation of her look was

one of the most problematic in the show's history to that date. As director Andrew Prowse says, "Who would think that a blue-skinned alien could be sexy?" When producer David Kemper told Dave Elsey that he was going to "introduce Scorpius's chick, I said fantastic. She's got to be as good as Scorpius. She's got to be a real evil character, and I knew exactly what I was going to do. I wanted her to be a weird sort of Spider Woman." According to Elsey, David Kemper wasn't convinced at that stage, and was anxious that the character looked like Claudia Karvan, who was playing her, and would be sexy.

"So I designed her as this blue, crustaceous character with spider legs on her head, and everyone looked at it, and went, 'Um... I really

don't know'," Elsey recalls. "We argued from beginning to end on Natira's look, but I kept trying to push it through. The thing is, while we're arguing about it, you've got to be doing it, otherwise it won't be ready for the day. The designs that we build normally are my very first designs, because that's all there's time for. Claudia came in and we cast her whole body. I talked to her about the character, showed her the drawings, and she said she couldn't wait to look like this. She thought it was the greatest idea ever.

"Lou Elsey designed the suit, then made it out of an experimental new fabric that she'd created — a Hot Flesh-fabric hybrid. Martin Izzard started sculpting the face to my designs. It was looking great and I really liked it, but still everyone else was worried. They wanted to have the spider legs fold up and lie flat on her head. I knew that what we'd built wouldn't do that, so we started working on a second head with the legs already folded in. We had it

ready with the costume for the make-up tests, got it together really quickly, put Claudia in it, put the lenses and the teeth in, put the head on with all the legs moving, and showed it to everyone. And they hated it!

"There was no way we could change it. I knew it was rough, because it was only the make-up test. So we got Claudia in the full costume on the day and she walked onto the set. And the whole place went quiet. Everyone looked at her — and suddenly reversed their opinions. We saw rushes the next day, and if it looked good on the set, it looked 200 times better onscreen. And everyone now uses that as a great example of what we can do on *Farscape*. It was a great make-up because it didn't completely disguise the actress — the character still looked like Claudia, as David Kemper wanted — and it was certainly sexy!"

The season finale, 'Die Me, Dichotomy', featured one of the Creature Shop's most elaborate creations: the Diagnosan, Tocot, played once again by Thomas Holesgrove. "I wanted him to be a really gentle kind of alien," Dave Elsey remembers. "Thomas had a muscle suit on, with rubber arms, and finger extensions, and we wanted to design a sort

Page 139: The crustaceous Natira.

Opposite page: Testing Natira's 'spider legs'.

Above: At work in the Creature Shop.

Next spread: The Diagnosan Tocot.

of Victorian doctor's outfit. We used a grey plastic material, and I love his legs and trousers, with the slashes. Then he had that big long neck with the ruffles on it, which made him look very gentle.

"Tocot is a rather sophisticated kind of being," Elsey adds. "The skull-like face that we designed for the character seemed to have a lot of life in it, even before we mechanised it. We normally know designs are going to work if they have that sense of life at the sculpting stage.

"Thomas was almost completely blind in it. There were holes that he could see through, but he only had a little bit of vision to the side, and virtually nothing in front, because of the wideness of the face. We also had to build a mechanical mask that fitted over the front. That was partly there as a plot point — to show what the character was like, and what his weaknesses were — but also because we thought it would be very theatrical to have Tocot's true appearance hidden for the first bit. Then there's the hatch in the mask that opens and reveals this horrible orifice in the face, and you don't know what it is... but it turns out to be his very sensitive nose! He also had glasses that came down when he operated, with little lights and magnifying lenses on them. They were kind of an old sci-fi idea, but done quite nicely."

Looking back, Elsey remembers the second season as an extremely challenging year for the Creature Shop: "But by the end of it, we had built up so much steam that we didn't want to stop. We thought: we can do anything now!" ■

CREATING PILOT

"Bringing Pilot to life was a real adventure in design and creation."

A ccording to series creator Rockne S. O'Bannon, the idea for Pilot, Moya's loyal symbiont and one of the most imposing creatures seen in the *Farscape* universe, "sprung from the Jim Henson Creature Shop maniacs. It was a design that was conceived in 1994 and was so instantly deemed cool, that it never really changed." The London Creature Shop's creative supervisor, Jamie Courtier, recalls that "we had some wonderful ideas about Pilot, and his little henchfolk, when we were doing design concept artwork for the ship. We had him with all these sockets plugged into the ship, surrounded by a 'motorway' system, with dozens of droids scurrying in every direction. There was constant traffic, his neural pathways reflected by radio controlled creatures on conveyor belts." However, even at that early stage, when *Farscape* was still known as *Space Chase* and was in development for the Fox network, budgetary constraints made themselves felt. "Our enthusiasm was suitably scaled down," Courtier adds. "I think we were hoping to indulge in one of the largest train sets in the world."

Pilot came into existence through the same process as do all the Creature Shop's projects: he started life as a drawing. "Pilot went through design evolution like anything else," Courtier says, "with different artists doing different drawings, looking at different angles of the character. Then we shared those ideas with Brian Henson and Rockne S. O'Bannon, and between ourselves as well. When we found out which ideas we all liked, we resolved our plans."

As the early design shows, Pilot did not always have his distinctive head shape. "He took one magnificent step forward when Kevin O'Boyle developed that big 'Sydney Opera House hat' look," Courtier remembers. "That was so striking, we stuck with it, and from that his environment changed and was scaled down. He was originally perceived as being a Pilot that people would visit far more than they do in the show. The original philosophy was that he was going to be huge."

As Pilot was being designed, the other main characters, including an early, insectoid version of Scorpius, were also being discussed. Pilot's claw arms owe their shape to the prototype of the Scarran-Sebacean hybrid. "As one of the key pitches to the networks, we had to do a Pilot model," Courtier says. "He's in the console, in situ. We were very rushed for time. None of us had really thought about what the arms were going to be like, but there were going to be eight of

Opposite page: One of the original design sketches for Pilot.

Above: *The finished maquette.*

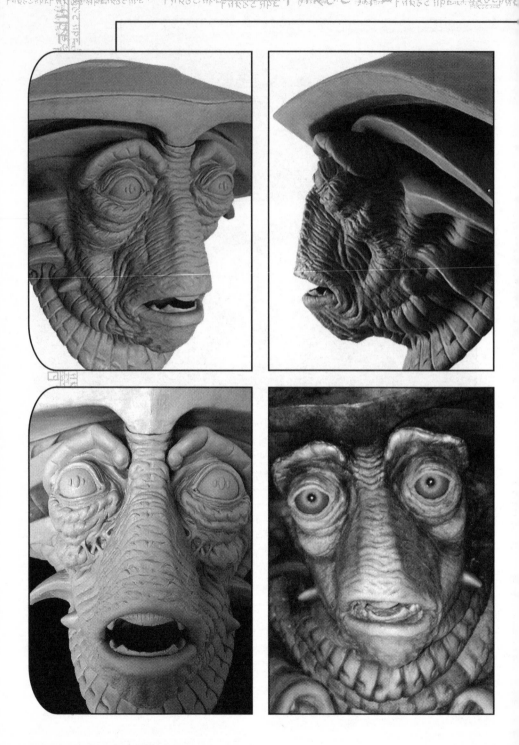

them. The prospect of modelling them was looming as a problem." The solution: cannibalise the maquette of the original version of Scorpius. "We held up a couple of little Scorpius arms and thought they would look absolutely great on Pilot. And that was his arms designed!"

Pilot's expressive, bulging eyes are a result of the ground-breaking design of his eyeplate, which is able to slide forward, while his fluid mouth movements come from the double jointing of his jaw. These were both additions that occurred once the show received the go-ahead, and the puppet was being created, following the design of the maquette.

The whole building process took around five months to complete in London. When the separate parts arrived in Australia, the Sydney Creature Shop's creative supervisor Dave Elsey had one major change to make. "We were trying to keep everything lightweight," Courtier explains, "so we used an aluminium stirrup to support the main gimbal. Unfortunately, that started to sag under the weight, so the stirrup was remade out of steel."

As the show has progressed, additional amendments have been made to Pilot's interior, allowing an increase in the versatility of the puppet, in particular more latitude of movement, for the second season.

The finished Pilot is about eighteen feet long and eight feet tall. The fibreglass skeleton is covered with a latex skin, and contains the control rods and apparatus with which up to seven puppeteers can operate him. Some are hidden underneath the console, while Sean Masterson, the head puppeteer, operates Pilot's mouth from a Henson Control System located a few feet away. Extra arms were created for use in close-up scenes. Although Sean Masterson voices him on the set, Pilot's distinctive voice is supplied in post-production by Lani Tupu. ■

Opposite page: *Pilot's incredibly detailed face, from the original sculpt to the finished puppet.*

Above: *Sean Masterson and Pilot discuss their next scene.*

Terry Ryan

> "The *Farscape* costume department has a motto: 'Comfort? What is comfort? What about confidence!'"

Terry Ryan's costumes have graced *Farscape*'s cast since its première. The Australian designer loves working on the show, and enjoys the challenges it brings. "*Farscape* is like a cross between a fairytale, a pantomime and sci-fi," he says. "It's not always hi-tech. That's what makes it interesting. It's all pretty labour intensive."

However, he doesn't see it as part of his job to change the lead characters' costumes too much. "I think there's enough other weirdoes coming in all the time! It would get pretentious if you started changing all the heroes," he points out. "They're heroes: they're always the same. Someone you can rely on."

Having said that, the second season does see John Crichton adopting a leather Peacekeeper outfit. "He's stopped being that IASA human," Ryan explains, referring to Crichton's original flight suit. "We surmised that everything he's got, he stole from Peacekeepers who came on board Moya. His clothes have become more practical for the life he's now living."

As with all the main cast's costumes, there are three sets of Crichton's leather outfit, ensuring that there is always one for filming and a back-up, while the third is being cleaned. There's quite a lot of leather to be seen in *Farscape*, and Ryan prefers working with the real thing, rather than synthetic alternatives: "It's organic. It moulds to people's shapes the more they wear it."

Aeryn's outfits have become a little more revealing as the series has progressed. "What's wrong with a bit of flesh?" Ryan asks. "Aeryn's become more feminine. She's lost that Peacekeeper fascist, Nazi thing and become more soft."

Zhaan's outfits also changed through the year, a highlight being her black, slinky outfit for the Depository

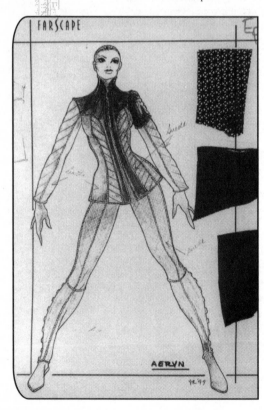

FARSCAPE

AERYN

raid in 'Liars, Guns and Money'. "The black patent leather gear for 'Out of Their Minds' was just Victoria's Secret sex shop gear," Ryan recalls, "but we made the black one for the 'Liars, Guns and Money' trilogy. That was fantastic, like Italian stretch vinyl. We had her collar and cuffs made by a jeweller — it was a bit hard for Virginia to wear."

Ryan admits that the producers give him a free hand with his designs. "The writers have ideas, but they're not designers. They can give you a personality or a character that you can take." A good example of this is Grunchlk in 'Die Me, Dichotomy'. "He needed pockets," Ryan says. "I thought, pockets? How pedestrian is that? So we designed a skirt that's a whole string of pouches. Instead of having a couple of pockets, we forced the idea and had this thing that's totally made up of them!"

As part of a team, Ryan ensures that his costumes match the work other departments are doing. "We help each other out," he explains. "For instance, the art department does all the leggings and armour; props do the guns, we do the holsters. We want them to look like they belong together. And I talk to the production designer, Tim Ferrier, about the sets, to make sure we've not done something purple when he's designed a lime green set. We talk before we go into a concept meeting, to make sure all the designers' heads are in the same space."

Opposite page: Terry Ryan's design for Aeryn in 'The Way We Weren't'.

Above: Grunchlk.

The actors' safety and comfort are prime considerations. Ryan created a special strengthened spacesuit helmet for the stunt work in 'Mind the Baby', so that Ben Browder wouldn't be at risk in the costume. "You've got to cover rigs for flying and that sort of stuff," Ryan adds. "The principals will probably have three costumes, and then a stunt costume with more holes for rigs. We're designing a lot of them now with openings for the wires built in. All you have to do is undo the fastenings and put the wires through, instead of having to wreck something every time you want to do a stunt. It's just so much easier for the actor than having to take it off, put on the rig and put it all back on again. When some of them have three hours of make-up, they don't want to spend an hour standing around getting changed."

FARSCAPE

VYNA

A location or set can inspire Ryan, as happened with 'Look at the Princess'. "They selected Sydney's Chinese Gardens," he recalls. "So we decided that everything should flow and look romantic. But then there were other characters in black leather and bondage gear amongst this peaceful, oriental sort of setting, which looked great!"

That look affected the costume for Francesca Buller as ro-NA. "I've got a bit of an oriental bent," Ryan claims. "Asians are all so wonderfully theatrical with their ceremonies. We wanted to make her alien, but didn't have time to have a wig or a prosthetic head made, so we used a skullcap. Francesca's got such a great face, with these great bones, so it worked a treat. Her costume had to fit in with the white and Chinese style, and we wanted her to be androgynous, but erring to the female side."

The simplest-looking costumes can cause a lot of work for the costume department. The feral youths in 'Taking the Stone', for example. "We wanted to have them nearly naked, but we couldn't because they had to have the rigs on," Ryan remembers. "Those costumes looked wicked, but they were hard to make. We wanted them to be skin-tight, but they had to be practical."

Similarly with the outfits for the other members of Chiana's race in 'A Clockwork Nebari': "They were very labour intensive, because they were all individually quilted. The fabric didn't have that much texture, so we had to stitch the texture into it. Because they wanted them really tight, but still be able to move, the costumes were in three sections so they were actually articulated — and very hot."

Ryan doesn't worry if his choices sometimes appear odd — he knows that somewhere, someone will work out a reason within the fiction of the *Farscape* universe. "You can get away with things," he laughs. "Justification is the name of the game." ∎

FARSCAPE

B'SOGG

Opposite page:
Terry Ryan's design
for Vyna in 'Taking
the Stone'...

Above: ... and B'Sogg
in 'Home on the
Remains'.

David Kemper

"Each year I have to do something that's more and more hideously insidious and then challenge Ricky Manning to find a way out at the start of the next season."

"TV has finally come up with a satisfying sci-fi hour." So wrote Diane Werts in the American *Newsday* magazine on New Year's Eve 2000, just before the final four episodes of *Farscape*'s second season swept onto American screens. Throughout the year, the series' profile had been raised ever higher. Huge posters of the main characters dominated Times Square in New York City to promote the beginning of season two. The show had taken off in countries all over the world, from Germany to India. Demand for new episodes was so great in the United Kingdom that the 'Liars, Guns and Money' trilogy and 'Die Me, Dichotomy' were given their world première on BBC2 in the first three weeks of December.

The merchandise began to pour out. *Farscape* action figures were released, and were praised for their incredible attention to detail. The first season's episodes were released on Region 2 DVD and video, selling more than 50,000 units. The Region 1 discs were released to equally good sales — in the first week, the Musicland Group were selling over 1,000 units per day, while 10% of Wal-Mart's video and DVD sales at that time came from *Farscape*. *The Illustrated Companion* to season one went into four printings to match the demand, and Boxtree published the first original novel in the UK, with more new titles announced for 2001.

Creation Entertainment launched the Official Fan Club at the first *Farscape* convention, held in Burbank, Los Angeles, at the start of August 2000. Over 600 fans filled the halls to greet many of the cast and crew, who had an opportunity to feel at first hand the love that Scapers have for the programme. Highlights included executive producers Rockne S. O'Bannon, David Kemper and Brian Henson regaling the audience with stories about the show's early days, and Anthony Simcoe giving a hysterically funny demonstration of how to produce D'Argo's distinctive tones. Simultaneously, an unofficial *Farscape* convention in St Louis was linked by video technology to a room at Burbank, so the fans in Missouri could join in the fun vicariously.

Ben Browder speaks for all his colleagues when he admits that he was humbled by the fans' response: "If there wasn't an audience, this show would not continue. We're as much beholden to them for our living and the great time we're having, as we are to anybody. If the fans don't tune in and they don't love it, we might as well pack our bags and go and look for another job. I feel grateful to them — they keep me employed. They can be grateful to me on the day I pay their bills! There's a huge amount of work that goes into the

show. We go to a convention and people are screaming for a few of us. But the fact of the matter is, our work is very much a product of hundreds of people saving our asses and bailing us out on a daily basis. There are the hands of, literally, hundreds of people on my performance. It's fun to talk about what I decided to do on set one day, but that's just one idea I had amongst thousands of ideas other people had."

Above: Season three's cast assemble.

Praise for the show flooded in, with an Australian television Logie Award nomination for Virginia Hey and success in reader polls by British science-fiction magazine *SFX* for Ben Browder, Claudia Black and Gigi Edgley, who was voted Best Newcomer. Make-up supervisor Lesley Vanderwalt was awarded the Australian Society of Make-up Artists Award for Best TV Drama for her work on the first season. Website SciFi IGN gave *Farscape* two prizes in its annual Bemmie Awards. Claudia Black walked away with Best Actress, especially noted for her performance in 'The Way We Weren't'. 'She's shown us the soft, funny and romantic sides of Aeryn without losing any of her hard-as-cinderblocks edge', the website enthused. And *Farscape*'s stunning CGI claimed the Best FX award: 'No other show on television truly makes you feel like you're actually in another world the way *Farscape* does.'

Post production on the second season continued into September 2000, when *Farscape* temporarily lost the use of its Homebush Bay studios to allow the BBC to cover the Olympic Games taking place next door. The third season eventually went into production in October, with filming beginning in November. Anthony Winley stepped up to replace Sue Milliken as producer of season three. "I suppose the loss of one featured character and the new ones to come will be the greatest thing about it," he promises.

"The show is continuing to get bigger," associate producer Andrew Prowse claims. "David Kemper's notion of keeping the show new and fresh, and taking on new challenges, is still going on. It won't be the same show. He has a definite plan for season three. My admiration for him is boundless. Sixty-six episodes is a phenomenal achievement. It's even harder in sci-fi, since you're not making something that has a formula. You're busting up the formula every time you create new worlds. You're in new situations every day."

Anthony Simcoe is looking forward to a resurgence of the tensions aboard Moya: "What separates us from other shows is that the main characters are at each other's throats! The key moments for me in *Farscape* are when we're chopping off Pilot's arm, or when Rygel is about to ditch everyone — when people are ready to sell each other out. It makes for much more interesting interaction between the characters. In season three we're trying to put the bite back into *Farscape*." Simcoe also hopes to be reunited with his favourite weapon. "I'm always looking for my big moment with 'Mr Sparky'," he reveals. "All the effects guys are coming up to me as if it's my decision and saying, 'Ant, come on, we want more 'Mr Sparky'!'"

As anticipation for the third season mounted, SCI FI in the USA presented a special season of reruns on the Friday nights preceding the season première on 16 March 2001. Six episodes were specially chosen by David Kemper, each 'essential' because they helped in some way to set the scene for the new year. Nicknamed 'Journey to the Centre of John Crichton's Brain', the reruns were designed as a crash course for newcomers, also providing veteran Scapers with some subtle hints about where the series was headed. Chosen were season one's 'Nerve' and 'The Hidden Memory', with 'Crackers Don't Matter', 'The Way We Weren't', 'The Locket' and 'Die Me, Dichotomy' representing the second year.

Series creator Rockne S. O'Bannon dropped some hints about the future in the accompanying notes on scifi.com. "One of the things that we want to do in seasons three and four is really examine the Peacekeeper world," he wrote. "The political scene and ramifications of that corner of the universe.

"In 'Nerve' and 'The Hidden Memory', Aeryn and Crais turn the first corner, the first serious corner, in their character development, something that we follow through in season two. Season three is going to take another, very big turn for them both, in particular for Crais. He will surprise us more than he has in the past.

"People seem to like Stark a lot and want to know more about him. So it was a really easy decision for us to bring him aboard in season two,

Above: Stark and D'Argo assist Crichton in the third year's opening episode, 'Season of Death'.

and he'll be very much a part of the cast and show in season three.

"We know our fans like to go back and watch our episodes again, so we wanted to lay in that foreshadowing lightly, in anticipation of the full-blown crisis later."

Even a week before 'Season of Death' heralded the start of the third year, Scapers were still reeling from Aeryn's death. Messages were posted daily to the bulletin boards worldwide from old and new fans. While inevitably there were those who doubted that Aeryn really had died, there were many mourning the loss of one of the strongest female characters in television science fiction. There were many other loose ends from season two still to be tied up, but it was that particular strand that Scapers everywhere were eagerly awaiting.

Asked to describe the new season shortly before it began, David Kemper said, "John Crichton sets a new goal for himself. A dangerous goal. An elusive goal. An obsessive goal. Scorpius will continue to be our villain, and we have some wonderful surprises for our audience. Rockne S. O'Bannon created a show out of his mind that was different and unique, and people responded to it. All we're doing is continuing to be different and unique in the spirit that he laid out for us." ∎

The language of the *Farscape* universe can be frelling confusing, even if you have translator microbes working for you. Here's a further A-Z selection to help you distinguish borinium from plok. Caw matan?

Adraxan vapour — highly flammable gas

Aliesan goat hole — a tight place: If he knows I'm around he'll lock up the Flax tighter than an Aliesan goat hole.

Amet — Litigaran equivalent of Amen

Bartantic — Hynerian insult meaning moronic or barbaric: Wait for me you bartantic Luxan!

Bendigan fire silk — very luxurious and sensual material, light as air, made into sheets for a bed

Bleethiks — animals analogous to parrots or monkeys, as in: They're chattering away like a pair of bleethiks.

Blez — relax or chill: Tell Moya she's just gonna have to blez out.

Borinium — a valuable resource found in ingot form and used as tradable currency

Brell marak — very precise unit of measurement: Down to the brell marak constant

Brell-phase — the part of the beginning of a wormhole (a proto-wormhole) which distorts when the wormhole collapses

Bristule — locked up or sealed tightly, as in: Bristule tight

Brocus histicalx — very rare pharmacological plant, the fruit of which Zhaan gathers from the Botany asteroid

Bym-ler — to kill, beat-up or thrash: Run a full blikka scan before I bym-ler the lot of you.

Caloric — a unit of power in Moya's transport pod

Caw matan? — slightly patronising turn of phrase, used by Rygel, meaning 'Do we understand each other?'

Cholok — Sebacean phrase indicating great exasperation, as in: For the love of Cholok

Cryostasis — method of containment in which a being, held upright in a box, is frozen or put into a state of suspended animation and is then readily transportable

Dekka — a measurement of space: Widen the pattern by dekka three

Dimensional schism — the interstices of time and space, when light and sound disjoin into base elements where Moya is stuck when StarBurst is not successfully completed

Drad — the best, wild or so amazing it will blow your mind, as in: The dradest

Dramalla — a flaccid creature like a jellyfish, as in: shaking like a dramalla sea jelly

Eachak — kind of Nebari fruit grown in an orchard

Electrinet — Litigaran method of containment using an invisible electronic web or net, which is thrown across the path of an escapee

Fa-pu-ta — Hynerian exclamation meaning 'like hell'

Frodank — term of derision denoting something stupid or ridiculous, as in: Your frodank idea

Frotein — refreshing drink, possibly alcoholic like a margarita

Garanta's brax — dismissive phrase meaning something worthless, as in: As if I give a garanta's brax

Garda — colloquial term used on the cemetery planet to indicate a male with a bit of attitude: He's no garda.

Gavork — aromatic medicinal herb, much prized by Zhaan for her apothecary

Grolash — mild insult, meaning moron or idiot, as in: I have reached my limit with this grolash.

Hamman — indicates left hand or port side. In general usage aboard Moya

Hingemot — Sebacean word for fool

Jick-tied — Sebacean equivalent of hog-tied

Jixit root — a herb, which is one of the most basic items in Zhaan's apothecary

Khan — personal insult questioning someone's parentage, as in: You frelling khan!

Kijrot — a mould Zhaan finds on the Botany asteroid, which is used to help heal D'Argo's broken bone

Kink — Litigaran term for hell: Who the kink you talking to?

Klemper — to alter, to push to an extreme: Of course, it might klemperise the system beyond tolerance.

Klendian flu — non-fatal flu, with all the usual coughs and painful symptoms

Krag's ass — term meaning 'I couldn't care less': I couldn't give a krag's ass

Limmok — tasty snack

Loomas — slang term for breasts

Macai — name of a dance, used as a euphemism for being trounced or humiliated, as in: You'd rather those trogs dance the macai all over our face?

Maddium steel — very tough, impregnable metal which can withstand a 'Metavek' explosion

MagCuffs — very strong Peacekeeper handcuffs

Maxzillian Pilatar Day Parade — possibly Luxan phrase indicating a very loud and rambunctious noise: Pounding like a Maxzillian Pilatar Day Parade

Melar gas — very potent knock-out gas made by Zhaan that suspends all bodily functions of those affected

Metra — measurement equivalent to a metre

Morna — hallucinatory mushrooms used in a version of Russian roulette. They have four heads to one stalk. When ingested, three are potent drugs, but one is fatal

Narl — a baby on the cemetery planet

Nashtin — very powerful cleansing pills, which are a great hangover cure but should only be taken one at a time

Nerve shot — one-off revival shot that is provided, with the one-off kill shot, in a Peacekeeper's supplies for use in emergencies upon themselves or a wounded member of their team

Nixar — colloquial term which indicates a female with a bit of attitude: No way nixar, you were quaking.

Nogelti — valuable crystals mined from the bones of the Budong carcass

Novatrin — a gas that is dangerous to Leviathans and is one of the six forbidden cargoes

Pemno — unit of measurement used to plot co-ordinates on a grid, as in: Delta six pemno nine lerg eight

Pewnkah — insult: Run by a pewnkah named Staanz

Plaking — panicking or getting antsy: Stop plaking.

Pleeking — messing or fooling around, possibly Nebari in origin: Come on, stop pleeking around!

Plintak — calming herbal medicine, made into lozenge form

Plok — Tavlek word for crap or bull: I'm sick of hearing your plok.

Razaric acid — powerful and deadly acid used by the Nebari in the collar they put on Pilot

Relkits — lowlifes, crooks or thieves: You slimy relkits

Renki — imp or cheeky upstart: You're an impatient little renki.

Repakkon — Luxan birthright ceremony, an important coming of age ritual

Sakman — unit of measurement of mass: 180 lbs = 0.000157 sakmans

Satra — mild swear word meaning hell

Sentra device — a shield that Traltixx promises will hide Moya from Scorpius, which programs itself to the inverse of the power drive

Shaltan — swear word meaning 'bloody', as in: I've been screaming my shaltan head off!

Shilai — Quaran turn of phrase indicating someone not thinking straight, as if he has rocks in his head, as in: head full of shilai

Squag — term for hell: It's hotter than squag!

Stevva — crystals or powder used in making explosives

Tacrah — part of the Delvian Seek ritual

Tadek — tabletop game of strategy, not unlike chess with lights and noise, played with Machiavellian skill by Rygel for money and scored in hents or quardra-hents

Tarou — deity followed by Bekhesh the Tavlek by reading the Writ of Tarou (like the Bible)

Thoddo — jerk, bastard or fool

Tralk — very insulting term for a female, as in: That little tralk

Trellon oil — aphrodisiac oil of unknown origin

Trezog — insult meaning idiot or fool

Trill — airhead, fool: You vapid little trill

Trog — derisive term meaning bastard or idiot

Trox — spunk or chutzpah: You got trox, I'll give you that.

Tulan relish — a flavoursome addition for food, like chutney

Vector gappa — a vector on a spatial grid, defined as by longitude and latitude

Vigilar — traitor, deviant or double-dealer: That vigilar Scorpius

Yllirian — a cleric of strict religious beliefs, possibly Hynerian

Zaccus — small climbing plant with tiny leaves that is good for alleviating many minor ailments, such as headaches

Zannet — personal insult indicating treachery, possibly Sebacean in origin: You're a coward and a zannet.

Zelka — red alert, an emergency indicator

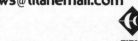